Spanish Grammar

HANDBOOK

PHIL TURK

Spanish Grammar Handbook

The Author:

Phil Turk is an experienced teacher, author of several Spanish language books and editor of *Vida hispánica*, the Spanish journal of the Association for Language Learning.

The Series Editor:

Christopher Wightwick is a former UK representative on the Council of Europe Modern Languages Project and Principal Inspector of Modern Languages for England.

Author's acknowledgement

I would like to thank José-Luis García Daza and Geneviève García Vandaele for their meticulous reading of the typescript and for some invaluable suggestions which I have incorporated into the text. Also my wife Brenda for her help with proof-reading and her patience and encouragement during the writing of this book.

Other titles in the Berlitz Language Handbook Series:

French Grammar Handbook	French Vocabulary Handbook ('94)
German Grammar Handbook	German Vocabulary Handbook ('94)
French Verb Handbook	Spanish Vocabulary Handbook ('94)
German Verb Handbook	
Spanish Verb Handbook	

CONTENTS

E   Linking and modifying meanings:
prepositions and adverbial expressions

F   Using numbers

G   Index

How to use this handbook

This *Grammar Handbook* can be used in two ways.

• If you want to get a general picture of some aspect of Spanish grammar, start with the introductory list of *Contents*. You can then read through the relevant sections of the text. The many cross-references will lead you to other, related topics.

• If you want to find out more about a specific grammatical point or about the use of particular Spanish words or expressions, consult the extensive *Index* at the end of the book. The *Index* has many sub-headings, and in addition items are frequently referenced under more than one heading. The *Index* will point you to individual paragraph numbers.

The *Handbook* gives a great deal of information about grammatical forms and structures, but above all is designed to show how they fit in with what you want to say or write.

• Grammatical terms are treated as convenient labels and used whenever necessary, but the *Handbook* does not assume that you already know what they mean. All the sections of this book include explanations of grammatical terms.

• A key feature is the number of examples, drawn from a wide stock of Spanish in current use. Wherever it makes sense to do so, these examples are linked together into a short dialogue, topic or narrative. If you do not understand a grammatical explanation, the example will help you to recognize the feature.

• This *Handbook* is intended for people who want to *use* their Spanish. Where constructions or expressions are used only in formal contexts, this is made clear in the text.

Finally, as a safety net, there are special warning sections wherever you see this sign, to help you avoid the more obvious traps and pitfalls.

A
PUTTING IDEAS INTO WORDS

1

1 Classes of words: parts of speech

1a   What kind of word is it?

It is often impossible to say what class a word belongs to (what *part of speech* it is) until it is used in a sentence. On the other hand, understanding a sentence may well depend on knowing what part of speech a word is, so it is useful to be able to recognize them. In this book we define each part of speech mainly by what it *does* – what it refers to and its function and position in the sentence. If you can also recognize it by its form, for example by its endings, then this is described as well.

1b   Content words and structure words

Four classes of word (the *content words*) contain most of the meaning of a sentence. The others (the *structure words*) do, of course, add to the meaning, but they do it mainly by the way they relate to the content words. The following table shows the two groups, with their English and Spanish names, some examples and the paragraph number where they are first defined.

Note   There is some overlap between these two groups, but the distinction is useful all the same.

I   Content words

Full verbs: **verbos completos** [➤7a]

Me hospedo a menudo en los grandes hoteles, pero los *odio*. Me *ponen* nervioso.	I often *stay* in big hotels, but I *hate* them. They *make* me nervous.

Nouns: **sustantivos** [➤20]

Conozco un pequeño *hotel* en Córdoba que tiene ocho habitaciones con *cuarto de baño*, *televisor* y *balcón*.	I know a little *hotel* in Cordoba which has eight *rooms*, with *bathroom*, *television* and *balcony*.

Adjectives: **adjetivos [➤22]**

Las habitaciones son *sencillas*, pero muy *cómodas* y bien *amuebladas*. Y aquella pareja *simpática* siempre sirve una cena *enorme*.	The rooms are *simple*, but very *comfortable* and well *furnished*. And that *nice* couple always serves an *enormous* dinner.

Adverbs: **adverbios [➤26]**

***Ahora siempre* me hospedo *allí* cuando estoy en Córdoba, porque *también* es *relativamente* barato.**	Now I *always* stay *there* when I am in Córdoba, because it is *also* *relatively* inexpensive.

II Structure words

Auxiliary verbs: **verbos auxiliares [➤7b]**

***Acabo de* recomendar esta hotel a un amigo que *suele* preferir los hoteles de lujo. Me *ha* dicho que le *ha* gustado mucho.**	I *have just* recommended this hotel to a friend who *usually* prefers luxury hotels. He *has* told me that he *has* been very pleased with it.

Pronouns: **pronombres [➤23]**

Los dueños *me* dicen que el hotel es antiguo, y *yo les* creo. Es muy interesante charlar con *ellos*.	The owners tell *me* that the hotel is ancient, and *I* believe *them*. It's very interesting chatting with *them*.

Determiners: **determinadores [➤21]**

***Este* hotel es mejor que *todos los otros* hoteles que conozco. ¡*Algunos* hoteles son horrorosos!**	*This* hotel is better than *all the other* hotels that I know. *Some* hotels are horrific!

Prepositions: **preposiciones [➤25]**

El hotel está *cerca de* la empresa, que está *en* el centro. *Para* llegar a la oficina *antes de* las diez, puedo ir andando *sin* tomar un taxi.	The hotel is *near* the firm, which is *in* the center. *In order to* arrive at the office *before* ten, I can walk *without* taking a taxi.

Conjunctions: **conjunciones** [➤5a]

El hotel es muy práctico *y* barato, *pero* a veces está completo *cuando* llamo para reservar una habitación, *aunque* siempre tratan de guardarme una.	The hotel is very convenient *and* it's inexpensive, *but* sometimes it is full *when* I phone to reserve a room, *although* they always try to keep me one.

Exclamations: **exclamaciones** [➤24]

¡Qué hotel *tan acogedor*!	*What a welcoming* hotel!
¡Qué simpáticos son los dueños!	*How nice* the owners are!
¡Qué habitaciones *tan cómodas*!	*What comfortable* rooms!
¡Lo agradable que es todo!	*How pleasant* it all is!
¡Claro que volveré!	*Of course* I'll come back!

2 | Getting it down on paper: spelling and punctuation

2a   *Spelling and sounds*

This chapter describes the main features of Spanish spelling and punctuation. It does not deal directly with Spanish pronunciation, as attempts to describe sound on paper are more likely to be a hindrance than a help.

2b   *The Spanish alphabet*

The order in which letters are listed in Spanish dictionaries is as follows.

Letter	Name of letter in Spanish	Letter	Name of letter in Spanish
A a	a	N n	ene
B b	be	Ñ ñ	eñe
C c	ce	O o	o
Ch ch	che	P p	pe
D d	de	Q q	cu
E e	e	R r	ere
F f	efe	S s	ese
G g	ge	T t	te
H h	ache	U u	u
I i	i	V v	uve
J j	jota	W w	uve doble
K k	ka	X x	equis
L l	ele	Y y	i griega
Ll ll	elle	Z z	ceda or ceta
M m	eme		

The combinations **CH** (**che**), **LL** (**elle**) and **Ñ** (**eñe**) are treated as letters in their own right in Spanish, and occur in the alphabet as noted above, even within a word, so **almorzar** (have lunch) would occur before **allí** (there) and **antiguo** (ancient) before **año** (year).

Because **B** and **V** are pronounced the same, to avoid confusion, **B** is called **be** and **V uve**.

K and **W** are infrequent. **K** is mainly used in the metric measure **kilo** and imported words (**kaki, kamikaze**), **W** in imports from English (**walki-talki, whisk(e)y, windsurfing**).

2c   The main spelling rules

(i)   Stress and the acute accent

The main accent used in Spanish is the acute (´), which is used *only* to indicate *stress*, and does not affect the actual sound of a vowel. Stress is the stronger emphasis which is put on one syllable of a word of two or more syllables, as also happens in English.

mantequilla	butter
margarina	margarine (U.S.), margarine (U.K.)
azúcar	sugar

There are three rules governing the position of the stress in a Spanish word.

(A) Words ending in a vowel, or **-n** or **-s** are stressed on the next to last syllable (**n** and **s** are included as they are often the last letter of verb endings and the plural of adjectives and nouns [▶19, 20g, 22a(i)]).

cosa	thing	cosas	things
agua pura	pure water	aguas puras	pure waters
hablo	I speak	hablas	you speak
habla	he/she speaks	hablan	they speak

(B) Words ending in a consonant except **-n** or **-s** are stressed on the last syllable.

arroz	rice
comer	to eat
reloj	clock, watch

(C) Words which do not conform to either of the two preceding rules have an accent on the stressed vowel.

azúcar	sugar
almíbar	syrup
hablaré, hablarás, hablará,	I, you, he, she, you, they will speak
hablaréis, hablarán	

This category includes all words with the stress two or more syllables from the end, including imperatives [▶15], infinitives [▶10a] and gerunds [▶10b] when object pronouns [▶23b] are added.

fant**á**stico	fantastic
aut**é**ntico	authentic
d**í**melo, d**í**gamelo	tell me it
dec**í**rtelo	to tell you it
dici**é**ndotelo	telling you it

 Certain groups of words have an accent in the singular and not in the plural, and vice versa.

Words ending in **-án**, **-én**, **-ín**, **-ón**, **-ún**, **-és**:

reh**é**n	reh**e**nes	hostage(s)
estaci**ó**n	estaci**o**nes	station(s), season(s)
ingl**é**s	ingl**e**ses	English

Words ending in *-en* stressed on the next to last syllable.

ex**a**men	ex**á**menes	exam(s)
or**i**gen	or**í**genes	origin(s)

The stress accent is also used as follows.

(A) On the stressed syllable of all interrogative (question) words.

¿Qu**é**?	What?
¿Qui**é**n?	Who?

etc. [▶6d, 23g]

(B) Although not strictly necessary, on the pronoun forms of the demonstratives [▶23h].

éste y **é**se	this one and that one

(C) To distinguish two words otherwise spelled the same.

de	of, from	d**é**	give (present subjunctive)
el	the (masculine)	**é**l	he, him
mas	but	m**á**s	more
mi	my	m**í**	me
se	himself, etc.	s**é**	I know; be (imperative)
si	if	s**í**	yes; oneself
solo	alone	s**ó**lo	only
te	you	t**é**	tea
tu	your	t**ú**	you

(ii)   *Other accents*

(A) The tilde (~) distinguishes the plain letter **n** (**ene**) from the **ñ** (**eñe**).

| señor | Mr., sir |
| año | year |

(B) The diaeresis (**el diéresis**) ¨ is used only in the combinations **-güe-** and **-güi-** to indicate that the **-u-** is sounded.

| vergüenza | shame, disgrace |

(iii) Vowels

(A) **A**, **e** and **o** are termed *strong* vowels, **i** and **u** are *weak* vowels. When two strong vowels occur together, they are pronounced as two separate syllables.

| leo = le-o, lees = le-es | I read, you read |
| cae = ca-e, caen = ca-en | he, she falls, they fall |

(B) When a strong and a weak vowel, or two weak vowels occur together, they half-merge to form a *diphthong*, which is regarded as one syllable.

seis	six	Dios	God
siete	seven	ruido	noise
viuda	widow		

(C) In a combination of a strong and a weak vowel, an accent is needed to stress a weak vowel, even if an **h** occurs between the vowels.

día	day	aún	still
leído	read (*past participle*)	continúo	I continue
prohíbo	I forbid		

(D) **Y** is a consonant when it occurs between vowels (**mayo**, May), and must be used instead of **i** in a diphthong on the end of a word.

| hay | there is, there are | estoy | I am |
| ley | law | muy | very |

(iv) Single and double letters

For double vowels see *Vowels* above [➤2c(iii)].

One of the noticeable features of Spanish is the lack of double consonants. Only the following consonants can be doubled, and that is because their sound is different from the single consonant.

Ll is a separate letter from **l** [➤2b]. Compare the following.

lamer	lick	**llamar**	call

Rr is rolled much more strongly than **r**.

pero	but	**perro**	dog
ahora	now	**ahorra**	he/she saves

Nn occurs in adjectives beginning with **n-** which have the negative prefix **in-**: both **n**s are sounded.

negable	deniable	**innegable**	undeniable

Note   Also **perenne** (perennial)

Words beginning 'imm-' in English have **inm-** in Spanish.

inmediato	immediate

In **cc**, the first **c** is *hard* and the second *soft*.

acceso	access	**sección**	section

(v)   The effect of endings on spelling

Adjustments to the spelling are sometimes necessary when a noun, adjective or verb changes its ending.

(A) A change of verb ending or a plural form of a noun may require a change of written consonant in order to maintain the correct sound. **C** has to change to **qu**, and **z** to **c** before **e** or **i**.

sacar	to take out	**saqué**	I took out
empezar	to begin	**empecé**	I began [▶19e]
una vez	once	**muchas veces**	many times [▶20g(iii)]

The following table shows the written combinations of consonant plus vowel after the sounds **k**, **kw**, and **th** (pronounced as 'th' in Spain, but as 's' in Spanish America).

Vowel	*Consonant*		
	k	**kw**	**th/s**
a	ca	cua	za
e	que	cue	ce
i	qui	cui	ci
o	co	cuo	zo
u	cu	-	zu
			-z (*final*)

The table on the next page shows the sounds **g**, **gw** and **j** (as in **aJo**) plus vowel.

Vowel	Consonant		
	g	**gw**	**j**
a	ga	gua	ja
e	gue	güe	ge/je
i	gui	güi	gi/ji
o	go	guo	jo
u	gu	–	ju
			-j *(final)*

In the combinations -**ce** and -**ci**, -**c**- *must* be used, *not* -**z**-, but -**ge**/-**gi** and -**je**/-**ji** are both possible.

(B) In the various verb tenses [➤18,19], the stress itself may change, so care is needed as to whether the changed stress creates the need for an accent.

hAblo	I speak	**hablAmos**	we speak/spoke
hablÓ	he/she spoke	**hablarÁ**	he/she will speak

(C) Some nouns and adjectives have an accent in the masculine singular and not the feminine or plural, or vice versa [➤2c(i) above].

(vi) *Use of capital letters*

Proper names, places and countries [➤20c] are spelled with an initial capital letter, and sentences always begin with a capital, as in English.

Juan y Mercedes son de Zaragoza   Juan and Mercedes are from
en España.   Zaragoza in Spain.

However, adjectives denoting region or nationality [➤22a(i)], titles [➤21c(v)] and days and months [➤30a, b] are spelled *without* a capital letter.

2d *Punctuation*

(i) *The main punctuation marks in Spanish:*

.	**punto**	period, full stop
.	**punto y aparte**	period/full stop + new paragraph
,	**coma**	comma
:	**dos puntos**	colon
;	**punto y coma**	semi-colon
¿	**ábranse puntos de interrogación**	open question marks

?	**ciérrense puntos de interrogación**	close question marks
¡	**ábranse puntos de admiración**	open exclamation marks
!	**ciérrense puntos de admiración**	close exclamation marks
(	**ábranse paréntesis**	open parentheses, brackets
)	**ciérrense paréntesis**	close parentheses, brackets
«	**ábranse comillas**	open quotation marks
»	**ciérrense comillas**	close quotation marks
—	**raya**	dash
-	**guión**	hyphen

(ii)   *¿? ¡!*

One of the most distinctive visual features of written Spanish is the inverted question or exclamation mark at the beginning of a question or exclamation. These are necessary since the subject pronoun [▶23b(i)] is often not expressed and therefore the verb and subject cannot be inverted as in English. The inverted question or exclamation mark is placed *at the beginning of the question or exclamation*, not necessarily at the beginning of the sentence.

| **Lo que quiero saber es ¿vamos a hacerlo? ¡No tengo ni idea!** | What I want to know is *are we going to do it? I've no idea!* |

(iii)   —

The **raya**, or long dash, is used in Spanish to introduce direct speech, where English would use quotation marks. It is always placed at the beginning of direct speech, and at the end if followed by unspoken words.

| **— Lo que quiero saber — dijo Miguel — es ¿vamos a hacerlo o no?** **—¡ No tengo ni idea! — respondió su compañero.** | "What I want to know," said Michael, "is are we going to do it or not?" "I've no idea!" replied his companion. |

The **raya** ia also often used where English uses parentheses (brackets).

| **Su compañero — que no era muy valiente — dudaba.** | His companion (who was not very brave) was hesitating. |

Parentheses ( ) may also be used in the same way.

(iv)   « »

Comillas, rather like the French guillemets, are usually used to quote from texts or foreign expressions, or to enclose titles.

Miguel se consideraba muy **«*avant-garde*».**	Michael considered himself very '*avant-garde*'.

(v)   –

The **guión** or hyphen is not greatly used in Spanish except to divide a word which runs over two lines of the page. Care should be taken to ensure that a new syllable begins with a consonant whenever possible. The months of the year hyphenated should give a good idea of how division into syllables and hyphenation works in Spanish: **e-ne-ro, fe-bre-ro, mar-zo, a-bril, ma-yo, ju-nio, ju- lio, a-gos-to, se-tiem-bre, oc-tu-bre, no-viem-bre, di-ciem-bre.**

The hyphen is seldom used in compound words, which are usually written as one word...

abrebotellas   bottle-opener

... although when two nouns are coupled, a hyphen is used [►3a(ii)].

bebé-probeta   test-tube baby
coche-restaurante   restaurant-car

Linking ideas together

3a   Compound words or phrases?

All languages need ways of combining word meanings so as to express more complex ideas. Especially in the case of nouns [➤20] and to some extent verbs [➤7], this may be done either by joining two words together to form one compound word or by linking separate words to form phrases.

(i)   Compound words without a hyphen

Spanish has quite a number of compound nouns of which the first element is a verb. These are written as one word, are masculine, and those ending in **-s** do not have a plural form.

abrebotellas	bottle-opener
abrelatas	can/tin-opener
espantapájaros	scarecrow
lavaplatos	dishwasher
lavavajilla	dish-washing/washing-up liquid
limpiabotas	shoeshine boy/bootblack
limpiaparabrisas	windshield wiper/windscreen wiper
parabrisas	windshield/windscreen
parachoques	fender/bumper (on vehicle)
portaaviones	aircraft carrier
portavoz	spokesperson
rascacielos	skyscraper
reposabrazos	armrest
sacacorchos	corkscrew

(ii)   Compound words with a hyphen

The hyphen is rarely used in this way in Spanish [➤2d(v) above], but two places where it does occur are as follows.

(A) Where two nouns are linked together and the second one describes or defines the first.

bebé-probeta	test-tube baby
camión-tanque	truck/tanker-lorry
coche-cama	sleeping car
coche-comedor	restaurant/dining-car
coche-patrulla	patrol car
comida-merienda	picnic lunch

(B) In compound 'jargon' adjectives such as the following, although they are often spelled as one word.

socio-político   socio-political

(iii)   Compound phrases

In general, however, it is not possible in Spanish to use a noun to describe another in the same way as English does in such phrases as *tea cup*, *team game*, *school year*. It is usually necessary to use a noun phrase joined by a preposition [➤20b] or to create an adjective: **taza de/para té**, **juego de equipo**, **año escolar**.

(A) If the object is destined for an action, **de** + the verb infinitive is used: **agujas de hacer calceta** (knitting needles).

Some examples of compound phrases with a preposition:

cordones de zapatos	shoelaces
cuchara de sopa	soup spoon
cucharilla de café	coffee spoon, teaspoon
equipaje de mano	hand-luggage
estufa de gas	gas-fire
libro de biblioteca	library book
máquina de coser	sewing machine
mina de carbón	coal-mine
la plaza del pueblo	the village square
vaso de/para cerveza	beer glass

Although the commonest link preposition is **de**, if a use or contents are indicated, other more specific prepositions, such as **para** (for) or **con** (with) may be used to avoid ambiguity. **Una taza de té** could mean either *a tea cup* or *a cup of tea*; **una taza para té** is *a cup for tea*, i.e. *a tea cup* and **una taza con té** is *a cup with* – i.e. containing – *tea* –*a cup of tea* [➤25].

(B) Sometimes, and especially in modern journalism, an adjective is formed and used. There is no hard-and-fast rule as to when an adjective should be used and how it should be formed, although the examples below contain the common adjectival suffixes **-ar**, **-ario**, **-al** and **-ivo** [➤22e].

año escolar	school year
crisis bancaria	banking crisis
estudios universitarios	university studies
frase nominal	noun phrase
frase verbal	verb phrase

política defensiva	defense policy
programas televisivos	television programs

Durante mis *estudios universitarios* se habló a menudo de una *crisis bancaria* en los *programas televisivos*.	During my *university studies* they often talked about a *banking crisis* on *television programs*.

3b   Suffixes

Suffixes are endings that you add to a word to modify its meaning or sometimes to convert it to another part of speech. Spanish uses a large number of them.

(i)   *Making adjectives from nouns*

A descriptive adjective is often formed by adding **-oso** to a noun. It often corresponds to the English suffixes '-y' and '-ous'.

arena	sand	**arenoso**	sandy
chiste	joke	**chistoso**	witty
furia	fury	**furioso**	furious
roca	rock	**rocoso**	rocky

Las playas de esta región son más arenosas que rocosas.	The beaches in this area are more sandy than rocky.

Where the noun itself needs to be converted into an adjective in order to describe another noun, the endings **-al**, **-ar**, **-ario**, **-ero**, **-ivo** are variously used, as described in 3a(iii) above. Unfortunately no firm rules can be given as to which ending suits which noun, and students are advised to learn each one as they encounter it or to use a noun phrase [➤3a(iii)].

(ii)   *Making verbs from nouns or adjectives*

One common way of creating a verb from a noun or adjective is to use the infinitive ending **-ear**, which produces a regular **-ar** verb [➤18a(i), 19a].

amarillo	yellow	**amarillear**	to yellow
el boicot	boycott	**boicotear**	to boycott
la chispa	spark	**chispear**	to spark, sparkle
la maña	skill	**mañear**	to act shrewdly

el toro	bull	**torear**	to fight bulls
el verano	summer	**veranear**	to take one's summer vacation/ holidays
verde	green	**verdear**	to turn green

There is also a related noun ending **-eo** which denotes the on-going process or activity.

el boicoteo	boycotting
el papeleo	paperwork, red tape
el toreo	bull-fighting
el veraneo	vacationing/holidaying

Por eso veraneamos aquí. Es una manera de escaparse del papeleo de la oficina.	That's why we take our vacations here. It's a way of escaping the office paperwork.

(iii) Diminutives and augmentatives

Spanish has a variety of suffixes which are added to nouns and sometimes adjectives to indicate smallness or largeness, but which often also contain further nuances. They take their gender according to that of the original noun or the noun they describe.

(A) The most generally used diminutive is **-ito** (or **-cito** or **-ecito**) which indicates both smallness and endearment.

Tenemos una *casita* cerca de la playa. Está en un *pueblecito* típico de la región. La casa es *pequeñita*.	We have a *little house (cottage)* near the beach. It's in a *little village* typical of the area. The house is *tiny*.

(B) Other diminutives are **-illo** (**-cillo**, **-ecillo**), **-ico** (**-cico**, **-ecico**), **-uelo** (**-zuelo**), which usually denote insignificance or unimportance.

Hay una *tiendecilla* en la *callejuela* que lleva a la plaza.	There's a *tiny little shop* in the *alley* leading to the square.

(C) The suffixes **-aco**, **-uco**, **-ucho** are pejorative and denote smallness and ugliness or unattractiveness.

¡Es una casucha!	It's a hovel!

(D) Augmentative suffixes **-ón/-ona** and **-ote/-ota** denote large-ness but often awkwardness or unpleasantness.

María, eres una *cabezota*. ¡No seas tan *mandona* y no digas *palabrotas*!	Mary, you're a *bighead*. Don't be so *bossy* and don't use *swearwords*!

(E) The suffix **-udo** added to a part of the body denotes size or volume.

orejudo	having big ears
peludo	hairy

(F) **-azo** can be augmentative or pejorative, but also has the intriguing meaning of *a blow with*.

Murió de un *balazo*.	He died of a *bullet wound*.
El delantero le dio un *rodillazo* a su adversario.	The forward *kneed* his opponent.

(The abortive 1981 coup d'état in Spain, led by Colonel Tejero, is often referred to as **el tejerazo** – *the coup by Tejero*.)

3c *Side by side: words in apposition*

Sometimes we add a phrase immediately after the names of people or things, giving further information about them. This explanatory phrase is said to be *in apposition* to the name.

In Spanish, a noun in apposition is not normally preceded by either the definite [➤21c] or indefinite article [➤21e].

Bogotá, capital de Colombia, es una ciudad muy poblada. *Tejero, autor del golpe fracasado*, fue condenado a la cárcel.	*Bogotá, the capital* of Colombia, is a highly populated city. *Tejero, the perpetrator of the failed coup*, was sentenced to prison.

B
PUTTING A SENTENCE
TOGETHER: SYNTAX

Recognizing sentences

4a   What is a sentence?

A sentence is a spoken or written utterance which has a *subject* and a *predicate*. When talking, we often say things which are not sentences (for example exclamations [➤24] or isolated phrases which make perfect sense because we know the context) but in writing we usually use complete sentences. The way a sentence is put together is known as its *syntax*.

4b   The subject of a sentence

(i)   Generally speaking, the subject is the word or phrase whose action or state the sentence is describing. In other words, it answers the question **¿Quién/Qué es/está...?** (Who/What is...?) or **¿Quién/Qué hace...?** (Who/What is doing...?).

Esta mujer **es mi hermana.** *Mi hermana* **vive en Guadalajara.** *Su casa* **está en las afueras de la ciudad.**	*This woman* is my sister. *My sister* lives in Guadalajara. *Her house* is on the outskirts of the town.

In Spanish, subject pronouns (**yo**, **tú**, **él**, **ella**, etc. – I, you, he, she, etc.) [➤23b(i)] are not often used, since the subject is expressed by the verb ending.

Esta mujer **es mi hermana.** *Vive* **en Guadalajara.**	*This woman* is my sister. *She lives* in Guadalajara.

The impersonal subject *it* is also often contained in the verb in Spanish [➤8h].

Es evidente que Guadalajara es bonita – cuando no llueve.	It is obvious that Guadalajara is pretty – when it is not raining.

(ii)   If the verb is passive [➤17] then the subject answers the question **¿A quién o a qué fue hecho?** (To whom or to what was it done?).

Su casa fue construida en las afueras de Guadalajara.	*Her house was built* on the outskirts of Guadalajara.

(iii)   In commands, the *informal* 'you' (**tú, vosotros**) is not normally expressed, though the *formal* 'you' (**usted, ustedes**) is often put in for clarity [➤15b, 16a, 18d(i)].

Ven/venid a vernos a Guadalajara (*informal*). *Venga usted/vengan ustedes* a vernos a Guadalajara (*formal*).	Come and see us in Guadalajara.

4c   The predicate of a sentence

The predicate consists of the whole of the rest of the sentence, excluding the subject. It must have at least a main verb (that is, a verb in a tense, usually in the indicative [➤18c(i)]. This verb *agrees* with the subject, that is, its form changes to match the subject. Chapter 7 describes the various types of verb and what they do.

Mi hermana *llegó*.	My sister *arrived*.

However, most predicates have more than this minimum, for example they may contain objects of the verb [➤8e,f], adverbial expressions [➤26] or non-finite verbs [➤10].

Mi hermana *llegó a Guadalajara*. *Compró una nueva casa en las afueras de la ciudad para estar cerca de su trabajo*.	My sister *arrived in Guadalajara*. She *bought a new house on the outskirts of the town so as to be near her job*.

4d   Types of sentence

There are three types of complete sentence:

• statements, which are the basic form;
• direct questions [➤6];
• commands [➤15].

All three must have a main clause; they may also have any number of subordinate clauses.

4e   Main clauses

A main clause is a sentence which can stand by itself, though of course it may not make sense unless you know what the speaker is talking about. The most common word order is subject + verb + object or complement, although other orders are possible in Spanish [➤4g], and object pronouns [➤23b(ii), (iii)] precede the verb in most circumstances.

Mi hermana no sabía.	My sister didn't know.

4f   Subordinate clauses

A subordinate clause is always dependent on another clause, whose meaning it completes or expands. It is linked to the main clause by one of three types of word:

• a subordinating conjunction [➤5a(ii)];
• a question word [➤6d];
• a relative pronoun [➤23k].

In certain subordinate clauses in Spanish, the verb will be in the subjunctive [➤16].

In the following example the subordinate clauses are in italics.

Mi hermana no sabía *dónde quería vivir porque iba a trabajar a Guadalajara, que está bastante lejos de nosotros.*	My sister didn't know *where she wanted to live because she was going to work in Guadalajara, which is quite a long way from us*.

4g   The order of words

Word order is very fluid in Spanish and is often varied according to the word or part of the sentence that the speaker wishes to emphasize. The following can therefore only be guidelines: there are no hard-and-fast rules.

(i)   *Subject + verb + object + adverbials*

This order gives a neutral statement, with no particular emphasis on any element. Adverbials of time tend to come before those of place, although this may also depend on the emphasis the speaker intends.

| Mi hermana compró una casa el año pasado en Guadalajara. | My sister bought a house last year in Guadalajara. |

(ii) Verb + subject

However, the subject often follows the verb.

| Ahora dice mi hermana que tiene una casa bonita. | Now my sister says she has a nice house. |
| Es cómoda la casa. | The house is comfortable. |

(iii) Any element of the sentence which needs to be highlighted may be brought forward to the beginning of the sentence, including the direct or indirect object, which has to be duplicated by the redundant object pronoun [➤23b(v)].

| *La casa* la compró mi hermana el año pasado. | My sister bought *the house* last year. |
| *El año pasado* mi hermana compró una casa en Guadalajara. | *Last year* my sister bought a house in Guadalajara. |

(iv) Adverbials

Adverbials tend to be placed immediately before or after the word they qualify, but the order may be changed in order to shift emphasis.

Mi hermana compró una casa en Guadalajara el año pasado.	My sister bought a house in Guadalajara last year.
Mi hermana vive ahora con su familia en Guadalajara.	My sister now lives with her family in Guadalajara.
Mi hermana vive ahora en Guadalajara con su familia.	My sister now lives in Guadalajara with her family.
Ahora mi hermana vive en Guadalajara con su familia.	Now my sister lives in Guadalajara with her family.
	etc.

(v)   Questions

In questions without a question word, the order is usually verb + subject + object.

¿Compró su hermana la casa este año?	Did your sister buy the house this year?

With **ser** and **estar** (be) [►8d], the complement is often put before the subject.

¿Es grande la casa? ¿Está contenta su hermana?	Is the house big? Is your sister pleased?

If the object or complement is shorter than the subject, the subject sometimes comes after it.

¿Tienen hijos su hermana y cuñado?	Do your sister and brother-in-law have any children?

In speech, the question is often indicated by intonation, and the word order remains as for the statement.

¿Su hermana compró la casa este año?	Did your sister buy the house this year?

Linking clauses together

5a Clauses with conjunctions

Conjunction means *joining*. There are two sorts of conjunction: *coordinating* and *subordinating*. Their names reflect their function in the sentence.

(i) Coordinating conjunctions

Coordinating conjunctions link clauses of equal status: main with main, subordinate with subordinate. They tell us something about how the clauses' meanings relate to each other (reinforcing, contrasting, etc.), but they do not change the clause structure at all.

These are the common coordinating conjunctions:

y	and
o	or
pero	but
no...sino (que)...	not...but...
entonces	and so
pues	so...
o...o...	either...or...
ni...ni...(no)	neither...nor...

La casa de mi hermana no es muy grande *pero* **es muy cómoda.**	My sister's house is not very big, *but* it is very comfortable.
No sólo **hay calefacción central** *sino que* **también tiene aire acondicionado.**	*Not only* is there central heating, *but* it also has air conditioning.
Ella nos dijo – *O* **tenemos una casa grande sin comodidades, o compramos una más pequeña** *pero* **con todo.**	She told us "*Either* we have a large house without amenities, *or* we buy a smaller one, *but* with everything".

 Sino (not **pero**) is used after a negative when the second phrase or clause contradicts the first. Used with a clause, it must be followed by **que** as in the second example above; it can of course be used with any part of speech.

Compró la casa *no* a una persona particular, *sino* a un agente.	She bought the house *not* from an individual, *but* from an agent.

(ii) *Subordinating conjunctions*

Subordinating conjunctions link subordinate clauses to the rest of the sentence. Usually the subordinate clause is the equivalent of an adverbial expression [➤26] – it answers one of the questions listed in paragraph 27b. Many of the following subordinating conjunctions require the verb in the subjunctive [➤16c].

(A) ¿Cuándo? When?

antes de que	before	hasta que	until
cuando	when	mientras	while, as long as
después de que	after	siempre que	whenever
desde que	since	una vez que	once
en cuanto	as soon as		

Mi hermana vivirá en aquella casa *hasta que* cambie de trabajo.	My sister will live in that house *until* she changes her job.
Mientras viva allí no la veremos a menudo.	*As long as* she lives there, we shall not see her very often.

(B) ¿Dónde? Where?

dondequiera que	wherever

Dondequiera que viva trataremos de visitarla una vez al año.	*Wherever* she lives, we will try to visit her once a year.

(C) ¿Cómo? How?

a condición de que	on condition that
a menos que	unless
a pesar de que	in spite of the fact that
comoquiera que	however, in whatever way
con tal que	provided that
sin que	without
si	if

A *pesar de que* viva tan lejos, nos llamaremos por teléfono.	*In spite of the fact that* she lives so far away, we shall phone each other.
¡La llamaré a ella *con tal que* me llame a mí!	I'll phone her *provided* she phones me!

(D) ¿Para qué? For what purpose?

de manera que	so that, in order that
de modo que	so that, in order that
para que	so that, in order that

Ya me ha dado su número de teléfono *para que* **la llame.**	She has already given me her phone number *so that* I can phone her.

(E) ¿Por qué? Why?

como	as
porque	because
puesto que	since
ya que	since

No podemos visitarla con más frecuencia *ya que* **todos tenemos que trabajar.**	We can't visit her more often *since* we all have work to do.

5b   Relative clauses

Relative clauses are introduced by relative pronouns [➤23k]. They describe or define a noun and thus do much the same job as an adjective [➤22]. The relative clause comes very soon (usually immediately) after the noun it refers to, for which reason the noun is known as the *antecedent*. When **que** is the object of the relative clause, the subject often follows the verb.

La casa *que compró mi hermana* **es muy cómoda.**	The house *that my sister bought* is very comfortable.

> **La casa _en la que vivía antes_ era más grande.** | The house _(that) she lived in before_ was bigger.

 'The house (that) she lived in.' Spanish cannot place a preposition at the end of the clause in this way, nor can the relative pronoun be omitted as in English [➤23k(v)].

5c Indirect speech

There are two ways of reporting what people have said (or perhaps thought). Both are introduced by verbs like **decir** (say), **contestar** (answer), **pensar** (think) or **creer** (believe). What is said is, in fact, the direct object of this verb [➤8e] – it answers the question **¿Qué dijo X?** (What did X say?).

(i) Direct speech

The first way is simply to repeat what was said or thought, i.e. _direct speech_. In writing Spanish, we would use the **raya** (–) where English uses quotation marks. The subject and 'reporting' verb are always inverted when they follow the words spoken.

> **– Voy a comprar una casa nueva – dijo mi hermana.** | "I'm going to buy a new house," said my sister.
>
> **– ¿Dónde vas a conseguir el dinero? – me pregunté yo.** | "Where are you going to get the money?" I wondered.

(ii) Indirect speech

The second way is known as _indirect speech_ or _reported speech_. You rephrase what was said in a clause, usually starting with the conjunction **que** (that) or a question word [➤6d]. You cannot omit **que** in Spanish as you can _that_ in English.

> **Mi hermana dijo _que_ iba a comprar una casa nueva.** | My sister said _(that)_ she was going to buy a new house.
>
> **Me pregunté _dónde_ iba a conseguir el dinero.** | I wondered _where_ she was going to get the money.

(iii) As you can see, direct speech is changed in several ways when it is reported in this way.

(A) Pronouns are changed so that they still refer to the right person. If a pronoun is the subject, the main verb is changed to match it.

(B) Verb tenses are changed, usually as in English, e.g. perfect to pluperfect, future to conditional.

– *He comprado* una casa nueva – dijo mi hermana. Mi hermana dijo que *había comprado* una casa nueva.	"*I have bought* a new house," said my sister. My sister said that *she had bought* a new house.
– *Compraré* una casa en Guadalajara – dijo mi hermana. Mi hermana dijo que *compraría* una casa en Guadalajara.	"*I shall buy* a house in Guadalajara," said my sister. My sister said that *she would buy* a house in Guadalajara.

A present subjunctive in a time clause in direct speech becomes an imperfect subjunctive in indirect speech, where the English merely changes from present to simple past [➤16c(i)].

– En cuanto *empiece* mi nuevo trabajo compraré una casa – nos aseguró mi hermana. Mi hermana nos aseguró que en cuanto *empezara/empezase* su nuevo trabajo, compraría una casa.	"As soon as *I begin* my new job I'll buy a house," my sister assured us. My sister assured us that as soon as *she began* her new job, she would buy a house.

5d   *Indirect questions*

Indirect questions are a form of indirect speech [➤5c]. They obey the same rules and are introduced by the same types of verb, followed by the relevant question word [➤6d]. Indirect yes/no questions [➤6b] and tag questions [➤6c], which have no question word, are introduced by **si** (whether). In this case, **si** may be followed by any tense which makes sense and is not subject to the rules governing 'if' clauses [➤16h]. The question words bear an accent in indirect speech, just as they do in direct questions [➤2c(i)].

Indirect questions are used for various purposes, including the following.

(i) *Reporting a direct question*

To report that a direct question has been or is going to be asked.

La pregunté *si* ya tenía el nuevo puesto de trabajo.	I asked her *whether* she already had the new job.

(ii) *Asking courteously*

To ask more courteously.

¿Podrías decirme *cuándo* empiezas?	Could you tell me *when* you start?

(iii) *Answering*

To say whether we know the answer.

No sé *quién* es su jefe.	I don't know *who* her boss is.

5e *Indirect requests and commands*

These are dealt with in Spanish sometimes by a construction with the subjunctive [▶16b(i)] and sometimes with the infinitive [▶8j(i), (ii)].

Le *dijimos que conprara/ comprase* la casa y ella *nos mandó* ir a visitarla allí.	We *told her to buy* the house and she *ordered us to go* and visit her there.

6 Asking for information: direct questions

6a What is a direct question?

A direct question is a form of direct speech. It tells us word for word what the person said or thought. The questions in the examples below are all direct questions – these are the actual words used, expecting a direct answer. But we often also talk about questions which have been or are going to be asked. These are indirect questions, which are discussed in paragraph 5d.

6b True or false? Yes/No questions

In this type of question we are asking whether something is true or not, so it is always possible to answer *Yes* or *No*.

Normally the subject and verb are inverted in this type of question, leaving the rest of the sentence unchanged. See the section on word order [▶4g(v)] for more detailed observations.

¿Ha hablado mi hermana con el agente inmobiliario? –Sí.	*Has my sister spoken* to the real estate agent? –Yes.
¿Es simpático *este señor*? –¡ No!	*Is this man* pleasant? –No!

6c Checking up: tag questions

Tag questions are statements with a question *tag* added to the end which asks for confirmation of the statement. English uses an enormous number of tags, but in Spanish the usual all-purpose one is **¿verdad?**. In speech, **¿no?** is often used after a positive statement.

La casa de mi hermana es preciosa, *¿verdad?*	My sister's house is lovely, *isn't it?*
Tuvo suerte en comprarla por un precio tan bajo, *¿no?*	She was lucky to buy it for such a low price, *wasn't she?*
No hay muchas casas así, *¿verdad?*	There aren't many houses like that, *are there?*

6d   *Asking for details: question-word questions*

We use these questions when we want to find out more about something we already know. The questions always start with a question word, such as those listed below. As you can see, Spanish question words all have an accent on the stressed vowel.

Many of these question words are the same as or closely related to relative pronouns or conjunctions (which do not have accents) [▶23k]. Do not confuse them!

The questions in paragraphs 6d(i) to 6d(iii) are answered by some sort of noun phrase [▶20b].

(i)   *People: ¿Quién? ¿De quién? Who(m)? Whose?*

¿Quién le vendió la casa?	*Who* sold her the house?
– El agente.	– The estate agent.
¿Con *quién* fue a verla?	*Who* did she go and see it with?
– Con su familia.	– With her family.
¿De quién era? **– De un ingeniero.**	*Whose* was it? – An engineer's.

Con (with) and other prepositions must always precede the question word [▶25].

(ii)   *Things: ¿Qué? What?*

¿Qué tiene que hacer ahora?	*What* does she have to do now?
– Nada.	– Nothing.

(iii)   *Selection: ¿Cuál? ¿Qué? Which?*

¿Qué habitación es la más grande? **– La sala de estar.**	*Which* room is the biggest? – The lounge.
Y ¿cuál es el dormitorio de su hermana? **– El grande.**	And *which (one)* is your sister's bedroom? – The big one.

(iv)   *Definition: ¿Qué? ¿Qué clase (tipo) de? What? What sort of?*

¿Qué habitaciones tiene la casa?	*What* rooms does the house have?

– Una sala de estar, una cocina y tres dormitorios.	– Living room, kitchen and three bedrooms.
¿Qué clase de suelo tiene?	What kind of floor does it have?
– Tiene baldosas.	– It has tiles.

The questions in 6d(v) are answered by an adjectival phrase [➤22].

(v)   Description: ¿**Cómo?** What...like?

¿Cómo son las habitaciones?	What are the rooms like?
– Son pequeñas pero cómodas.	– They are small but comfortable.

The questions in paragraphs 6d(vi) to (x) are answered by adverbial expressions [➤26, 27].

(vi)   Time: ¿**Cuándo?** When?

¿Cuándo va usted a ver la casa? – Mañana.	When are you going to see the house? – Tomorrow.

(vii)   Place: ¿**Dónde?** Where?

¿Dónde vive usted? – En el centro de la ciudad.	Where do you live? – In the town center.

(viii)   Manner (methods and means): ¿**Cómo?** How?

¿Cómo va a ir? – En coche.	How are you going to go? – By car.

(ix)   Quantity and degree: ¿**Cuánto?** ¿**Cuántos?** How much? How many?

¿Cuánto tiempo tiene usted?	How much time do you have?
– No mucho.	– Not much.

(x) *Reasons: ¿**Por qué?** Why?*

¿*Por qué* no puede esperar hasta la semana que viene? – ¡Porque mi hermana me matará si no voy mañana!	*Why* can't you wait until next week? – Because my sister will kill me if I don't go tomorrow!

C
ACTIONS AND STATES:
VERBS AND THEIR USES

What verbs do

➤ For extensive treatment of the forms of Spanish verbs, see the *Berlitz Spanish Verb Handbook*.

7a   Full verbs

The very great majority of verbs tell us about the actions, state of mind or (possibly changing) situation of the subject of the sentence [➤4b]. These we call *full* verbs.

Me *hospedo* a menudo en hoteles grandes , pero los *odio*. Me *ponen* nervioso.	I often *stay* in big hotels, but I *hate* them. They *make* me nervous.

7b   Auxiliary verbs

A much smaller group of verbs is used almost exclusively to add something to the sense of a full verb, for example to make a compound tense or to add a comment on an action. These are called *auxiliary* (i.e. helping) verbs [➤9, 11c, 19c.]

He encontrado un pequeño hotel al que *he* vuelto varias veces. *Suelo* ir allí cuando estoy de negocios.	I *have* found a small hotel, to which I *have* returned several times. I *usually go (am accustomed to going)* there when I am on business.

7c   Dual-purpose verbs

Some verbs can be used either with a full meaning or as an auxiliary. In Spanish, the main compound tense auxiliary **haber** is used in the third person singular **(hay)** meaning *there is/there are*. There are also a number of verbs which are used as *modal auxiliaries*, or *modals* [➤9], which have a modified meaning when used in this way. When **querer** (want) is used with an infinitive, it expresses willingness to do something, and is the equivalent of *will*; **acabar** means *finish*, but used with **de** + infinitive it means *have just (done)*.

¿Quiere darme la dirección, por favor? – Sí claro. *Acabo de* dársela a otros amigos. *Hay* mucho interés por este hotel.

Will you give me the address, please? – Yes, of course. *I have just* given it to other friends. *There is* a lot of interest in this hotel.

8 | **What verbs govern**

8a   What does a verb govern?

(i)   Transitive and intransitive verbs

All sentences consist of a subject and a predicate. The predicate will consist of at least one main verb and, in most cases, further information. In the example below, the predicate consists of the main verb only.

Pedro *llega.*	Pedro *arrives.*

In this example, the predicate consists of verb plus further information.

Pedro *ha comprado un billete.*	Pedro *has bought a ticket.*

Since subject pronouns [➤23b(i)] are often not expressed in Spanish, it is possible for the subject and predicate, and therefore a complete sentence, to be expressed in one word.

Llega.	*He's arriving.*

When a verb can stand in a sentence without the necessity for further information to be given (as with **llega** in the above examples), it is called *intransitive*. When a verb requires a direct object [➤8e] in order to complete its sense, as with **ha comprado** in the above example, the verb is called *transitive*. **Ha comprado** by itself would not make sense.

(ii)   Some verbs can be used transitively or intransitively.

Pedro escribe.	Pedro is writing.
Pedro escribe *una carta.*	Pedro is writing *a letter.*

(iii)   The predicate may contain a great deal of optional information, i.e. information which, though useful, is not necessary for the verb to perform its grammatical function.

> **Pedro ha comprado un billete *para*** Pedro has bought a ticket *for the five*
> ***el vuelo de las cinco de la tarde.*** *p.m. flight.*

In the above example, the verb **ha comprado** requires **un bi-llete** as its direct object to complete its sense, but all the remaining information in the predicate, though it may be useful or important, does not affect the grammatical completeness of the sentence.

 Spanish verbs may well be linked to their objects or other parts of the predicate in a different way from their English equivalents [➤8i]. For example, a transitive verb in English, taking a direct object, may require a preposition before its object in Spanish.

> ***Gozamos de* buena salud.** *We enjoy* good health.

Some verbs taking a direct object in Spanish need a preposition in English.

> ***Escuchamos* la radio.** *We listen to* the radio.

Some take a preposition, but a different one in each language.

> **Como diversión, no se puede** As entertainment, you can't *rely on*
> ***contar con* la televisión;** the television; it *depends on* the
> ***depende de* los programas.** programs.

[For more details on these differences see paragraph 8i.]

8b   *Lone verbs: intransitive verbs*

(i)   *What is an intransitive verb?*

Intransitive verbs, therefore, govern no territory at all, though the sentence may, of course, contain adverbial expressions [➤26].

> ***Dormía* (profundamente) cuando** I *was sleeping* (soundly) when my
> **mis padres *llegaron* (en taxi).** parents *arrived* (by taxi).

(ii)   *Verbs used reflexively*

Many Spanish equivalents of English intransitive verbs are

used in the reflexive form [►8g], including many actions carried out on oneself, but not usually expressed reflexively.

La puerta *se abrió* de repente mientras *me afeitaba.*	The door *opened* suddenly while I *was shaving.*

The following is a selection of verbs which are used reflexively in Spanish as the equivalent of a verb used intransitively in English.

abrirse	open	**incorporarse**	sit up
acostarse	go to bed	**irse**	go away
afeitarse	shave	**lavarse**	wash
cansarse	get tired	**levantarse**	get up,
cerrarse	close		stand up
despertarse	wake up	**marcharse**	go away
dormirse	go to sleep	**zambullirse**	dive

8c   Verbs linking equals: the complement

A small number of verbs simply act as a link between the subject and another word or phrase, which is called the *complement* of the verb. Usually the complement is a noun phrase [►20], in which case it refers to the same person or thing as the subject.

Tanto mi madre como mi padre *son* músicos excelentes. Mi padre *parece* casi profesional y mi madre se ha *hecho* solista de concierto	Both my mother and my father *are* excellent musicians. My father *appears* almost professional and my mother has *become* a concert soloist.

The main Spanish linking verbs are as follows:

ser, estar	be
ponerse, hacerse, llegar a ser	become
parecer	seem, look, appear
sentirse	feel

8d   Two verbs 'to be': ser and estar

A distinctive feature of Spanish is having two verbs *to be*, which have their own specific uses and are not usually interchangeable.

(i) Ser

Ser is used with noun phrases to identify people and objects in answer to the questions **¿Quién?** (Who?) and **¿Qué?** (What?).

Mi padre *es músico.*	My father *is a musician.*
***Somos* una familia musical.**	*We are* a musical family.
Nuestro piano *es un Steinway.*	Our piano *is a Steinway.*

Ser is also used with adjectives and noun phrases to describe the basic, natural characteristics of a person or object in answer to the question **¿Cómo es?** (What [is he/she/it] like?) or **¿De qué es?** (What [is it made] of?).

Nuestro piano *es muy grande y de alta calidad.*	Our piano *is very large and of high quality.*
Es de hierro y madera.	*It's (made of) iron and wood.*

Ser is also used:

• To say where you are from

***Somos* de Barcelona.**	*We are* from Barcelona.

• To tell the time [➤29a]

***Son* las doce.**	*It's* twelve o'clock

• For dates [➤30c]

***Es* el dos de junio.**	*It's* the second of June.

• To form the true passive [➤17b, c]

El piano *ha sido* vendido.	The piano *has been* sold.

(ii) Estar

Estar, by contrast, is derived from the Latin *stare* (to stand), and is related to the word *state*. It is therefore used in answer to the question **¿Dónde?** (Where?, i.e. Where does it *stand?*) and **¿Cómo?** (How?, i.e. In what *state*?).

Estoy en casa hoy.	*I am at home* today.
Estoy de buen humor.	*I am in a good mood.*
Yo *estoy muy contenta* hoy porque acabo de aprobar mi examen.	I *am very pleased* today because I have just passed my exam.
Si hubiese suspendido mi padre *habría estado furioso* conmigo.	If I had failed, my father *would have been furious* with me.

Estar is also used:

• To indicate a state resulting from the action of some reflexive verbs [➤8g]

Mi padre *está muy cansado*.	My father *is very tired*.
Se cansa mucho estos días.	He gets tired a lot these days.

• For dates [➤30c]

Estamos a dos de junio.	*It's* the second of June.

• To form the progressive tenses [➤19c(i)]

Estamos aprendiendo.	*We are* learning.

• In the descriptive passive with past participle [➤17c]

El piano *está* vendido.	The piano *is* sold.

• In the phrases **estar para** (to be about to) and **estar por** (to be in favor of) + infinitive [➤8k(iv), (vi)]

Cuando *estábamos para* vender el piano, mi padre lamentó que no *estaba por venderlo*.	When we *were about to* sell the piano, my father complained he *wasn't in favor* of selling it.

• In another way of saying what something is made of: **estar hecho de**

El piano *estaba hecho* de madera y hierro.	The piano *was made of* wood and iron.

(iii)   Ser/estar + adjective

When the complement is an adjective [➤22], care should be taken to use the correct verb *to be*. **Estar** is used when the state is changeable or brought about by circumstances, **ser** when it is the predictable, natural characteristic.

Estoy cansada **después de tanto trabajo, pero aprobé el examen porque** *soy muy aplicada.*	*I'm tired* after so much work, but I passed my exam because *I'm very studious.*

• **Ser** is usually used with **joven** (young) and **viejo** (old).
• **Estar** is used with **muerto** (dead).

Mis hijos *son muy jóvenes.*	My children *are very young.*
Mis abuelos *están muertos.*	My grandparents *are dead.*

• An adjective denoting an attribute usually associated with **ser** is sometimes made more vivid when used with **estar**, especially in exclamations, and is often the equivalent of *look*.

¡Qué guapa estás!	How pretty you look!

Note   Some adjectives change their meaning depending on whether they are used with **ser** or **estar**.

ser aburrido	be boring	**ser divertido**	be amusing
estar aburrido	be bored	**estar divertido**	be amused
ser bueno	be good	**ser listo**	be clever
estar bueno	be tasty	**estar listo**	be ready
ser cansado	be tiresome	**ser malo**	be bad
estar cansado	be tired	**estar malo**	be sick/ill

8e   Verbs with one object: the direct object of transitive verbs

A very large number of verbs normally govern a noun phrase [➤20] which refers to whatever is primarily affected by the action of the verb. These verbs are *transitive*, and the noun phrase is the *direct object*.

Sé *leer* **la música pero no** *toco* **ningún instrumento.**	I can *read* music, but I don't *play* any instrument.

¡Pero en cambio *tengo* un ordenador!	I *have* a computer instead!

 When the direct object is a *definite* person or persons, the preposition **a**, called the *personal* **a**, is placed before the direct object. It has no literal meaning and is simply used as an indicator. It is sometimes also used before animals, towns and countries in order to personalize them [➤25e].

Todavía no conozco *al* nuevo novio de mi hija.	I don't know my daughter's new boyfriend yet.

➤ Transitive verbs used in the passive (Many computers *are manufactured* in the Far East) are described in chapter 17.

8f   *Verbs with two objects: direct and indirect objects*

Some transitive verbs describe the transfer of the direct object to another person (or possibly thing). This person is then the *indirect object* of the verb. The main uses for indirect objects are described in the following paragraphs.

(i)   *Transferring something or someone*

Verbs which describe the transfer of people, objects or information normally must have an indirect object if they are to make sense, though sometimes it may be assumed. Verbs in this group include the following.

dar	give	**explicar**	explain
decir	say, tell	**mandar**	send
describir	describe	**mostrar**	show
enseñar	teach, show	**regalar**	give (as gift)
enviar	send	**prestar**	lend
escribir	write	**traer**	bring, fetch

Mi hijito le *regaló* a mi marido un nuevo programa para la Navidad. Me *dijo* que era fácil, ¡pero tuvo que *enseñarle* cómo funcionaba!	My young son *gave* my husband a new program for Christmas. He *told* me that it was easy, but he had to *show him* how it worked!

Note   Often in Spanish, the indirect noun object is duplicated in the form of the indirect object pronoun, as in the first example above. This is known as the 'redundant object pronoun'. Grammatically it is not strictly necessary, but it is nevertheless frequently used in speech and sometimes in writing [➤23b(v)].

 In Spanish, indirect objects cannot become the subject of a passive verb [➤17e(i)] as they can in English (*She was given* a dictionary).

(ii)   A person as indirect object

Many activities involve another person. They may then have an indirect object which has the general meaning of *for X*.

Te **haré un pastel si *me*** **encuentras la receta.**	I'll make *you* a cake if you'll find *me* the recipe.

The person or thing from which something is separated is often expressed as the indirect object in Spanish.

Mi hijo compró el programa *a* **un vecino nuestro.**	My son bought the program *from* a neighbor of ours.

The following verbs also use this construction.

confiscar a	confiscate from	**quitar a**	take away from
llevarse a	take away from	**robar a**	steal from

Vamos a quitar el ordenador *a* ***nuestro hijo* si pasa demasiado** **tiempo delante.**	We're going to take the computer away *from our son* if he spends too much time in front of it.

(iii)   Actions to the body or clothes

When an action is performed to a part of someone's body or clothing, the person is the indirect object and no possessive [➤21c(v), 21g(vi)] is used

Me **operaron el pie.**	They operated on *my* foot.
El aceite *le* manchó la camisa.	The oil stained *his* shirt.

(iv)   Order of objects

When both direct and indirect objects are nouns, the direct usually precedes the indirect if they are of similar length. If one object is significantly longer than the other, the shorter comes first.

Mi hijo (le) regaló *un nuevo programa a su padre.*	My son gave *a new program to his father.*
Mi hijo (le) regaló *a su padre este magnífico nuevo programa de ordenador.*	My son gave *his father this wonderful new computer program.*

When both objects are pronouns, the indirect always precedes the direct.

Mi hijo *se lo* **regaló**	My son gave *it to him*/gave *him it.*

For the position of object pronouns in relation to the verb, see paragraph 23b(iv).

8g   *Objects which refer to the subject: reflexive verbs*

A reflexive verb is a transitive verb whose action is 'turned back' on the subject. The object therefore refers to the same person or thing as the subject.

(i)   Many Spanish reflexive verbs are the equivalent of English intransitive verbs [▶8b(ii)].

¡*Lávate* **antes de salir!**	*Wash (yourself)* before you go out!
Prefiero *afeitarme* **con jabón y agua.**	I prefer *to shave* (myself) with soap and water.

(ii)   Reflexive pronoun as indirect object

The reflexive pronoun can also be the indirect object [▶8f], particularly when the subject is performing an action to a part of his or her own body or article of clothing [▶8f(iii)].

Mientras limpiaba el coche *se* **manchó la camisa.**	While he was washing the car, he stained his shirt.

The reflexive pronoun is also used in a reciprocal sense, i.e. doing the action to each other, either as a direct or indirect object.

***Nos* visitamos cada año y *nos* escribimos cada mes.**	We visit *each other* every year and write *to each other* every month.

(iii)   Idiomatic reflexives

There are a good number of common Spanish reflexive verbs with idiomatic rather than literal meanings. Amongst these are verbs which denote *getting into a state*, and several verbs meaning *become*.

aburrirse	get bored	**preocuparse**	get worried
acostumbrarse	get accustomed	**hacerse**	become
enojarse	get angry	**ponerse**	become
extrañarse	be suprised, puzzled	**sentarse**	sit down, be seated
fastidiarse	get annoyed		

Mi mujer siempre *se preocupa* cuando llama la señora Pérez.	My wife always *gets worried* when Mrs. Pérez phones.

The subsequent 'state' is indicated by **estar** + past participle [➤8d].

***Yo estoy acostumbrado* a esto, pero *mi mujer está bastante preocupada*.**	I'm *accustomed* to this, but *my wife is quite worried*.

(iv)   Some verbs have no non-reflexive form at all.

arrepentirse	repent, be sorry	**dignarse**	deign
		jactarse	boast
atreverse	dare	**quejarse**	complain

– ¿Viene a *quejarse*? – pregunté.	"Is she coming to complain?" I asked.

(v)   Intensifying

Sometimes making a verb reflexive in Spanish can intensify the meaning.

beber	drink	**comer**	eat
beberse	drink up	**comerse**	eat up
caer	fall	**ir**	go
caerse	fall over	**irse**	go away

> **Primero *se bebió* una copa que mi mujer le ofreció.**
>
> First she *drank up* a glass of wine my wife offered her.

In Spanish, the reflexive verb is often used to avoid the passive [▶17e(i)].

8h *Impersonal and 'back-to-front' verbs*

An impersonal verb in English has the subject *it*, which has no real meaning by itself, but serves to introduce weather phrases and other verbs, in sentences such as *it is raining*, *it is impossible to tell*, etc. In Spanish, the pronoun *it* is, of course, contained in the third person singular of the verb and not expressed as a separate word. There are several types of impersonal verb.

(i) *Talking about the weather and natural phenomena*

There are a number of expressions which use **hacer**, a few with **haber**, and verbs such as **llover** (rain), **nevar** (snow), **amanecer** (dawn), etc. Some expressions after **hacer** need **mucho** rather than **muy** for *very*, as they are nouns, not adjectives.

llover	rain
nevar	snow
helar	freeze
amanecer	dawn
anochecer	get dark
hacer (muy) bueno/buen tiempo	be (very) good weather
hacer (muy) malo/mal tiempo	be (very) bad weather
hacer (mucho) frío	be (very) cold
hacer (mucho) calor	be (very) warm, hot
hay (mucha) niebla	be (very) foggy

> ***Es* invierno. *Anochece* temprano, *hace* frío, *hay* heladas y *va a nevar*.**
>
> *It is* winter. *It gets dark* early, *it's* cold, *there are* frosts and *it's going to snow*.

| Ayer *hizo mucho frío, llovió* e *hizo muy mal tiempo.* | Yesterday *it was very cold, it rained*, and *the weather was very bad* (*it was very bad weather*). |

(ii) Ago

Hace is also used meaning *ago* and is placed *before* the time phrase.

| *Hace* diez años, el invierno fue atroz. | Ten years *ago*, the winter was atrocious. |

Hace or **desde hace** are used to express actions which have or had been going on for a period of time and may well continue [➤12a(iv), 13b(v)].

(iii) *Haber* there is, there are

Haber is used in the third person – always singular – with the meaning *there is/there are*. The present tense has a special form **hay.**

| Ayer *había* agua en las carreteras. Hoy *hay* hielo. *Habrá* problemas para los automovilistas. | Yesterday *there was* water on the roads. Today *there is* ice. *There will be* problems for drivers. |

Hay que + infinitive (it is necessary to) [➤9b(ii)].

(iv) *Parece; Es imposible* It seems; It's impossible

Verbs such as **parece** (it seems), **es imposible** (it's impossible), although usually termed *impersonal*, are not strictly so in Spanish, as the following infinitive or clause is really the subject of the verb, as you can see if you turn the sentence around (the subject is in italics).

| Es imposible *pasar por esta carretera.* *Pasar por esta carretera* es imposible. Parece increíble *que no hayan puesto sal.* | It is impossible *to go along this road.* *To go along this road* is impossible. It seems incredible *that they haven't put salt down.* |

Que no hayan puesto sal parece increíble.	*That they haven't put salt down seems incredible.*

(v)   *Gustar* (like) *and similar 'back-to-front' verbs*

There is a group of verbs in Spanish which work the opposite way around to their English counterparts: the subject in English (usually a person) is the object in Spanish. The verb is usually in the third person. If the object (the person) is a noun, it usually comes first, preceded by the personal **a** [►8e] and duplicated by the *redundant object pronoun* [►23b(v)].

A mi hijo le gustan *los ordenadores*. **También le gusta** *el fútbol*.	My son likes *computers*. He also likes *soccer*.

The main points about this construction are therefore:

• The Spanish subject usually follows the verb, which is plural if the subject is plural: i.e. if you like something plural, the verb is plural. You are saying 'Computers please my son': '*they* please him'.

• A pronoun object is often reinforced by **a** + the disjunctive pronoun [►23f], especially for emphasis.

A mí no *me* **gustan los ordenadores.**	*I* don't like computers.

• Some other common verbs which work in this way are:

me apetece(n)	I feel like, fancy
me duele(n)	I've a pain in, my...hurts
me emociona(n)	I'm thrilled by
me encanta(n)	I love
me entusiasma(n)	I'm enthusiastic about, keen on
me falta(n)	I'm missing, I'm lacking
me gusta(n)	I like
me interesa(n)	I'm interested in
me queda(n)	I have left
me sobra(n)	I have...over, too much

A mi hijo *le sobran* las buenas intenciones, pero *le falta* la aplicación. Sólo le *quedan* dos meses antes de sus exámenes.	My son *has plenty of* good intentions, but *he lacks* application. He has only two months *left* before his exams.

- To say 'I like/feel like, etc. *doing* something', the second verb is in the infinitive [➤10a].

Me duelen los dientes pero *no me apetece ir* al dentista. *A mi hijo le encanta jugar* con su ordenador, pero *no le interesa lavar* los platos.	*I've got toothache*, but I *don't feel like going* to the dentist. My son *loves playing* with his computer, but *he is not interested in doing* the dishes.

- If the verb is influencing another person or thing to do something, the subjunctive is needed after **que** [➤16b(i)].

No nos gusta que pase tanto tiempo con su ordenador.	*We don't like him spending* so much time with his computer.

8i   *Verb + preposition + noun phrase: prepositional objects*

Certain verbs are linked to their object by a preposition. In this case, the preposition does not usually have its full meaning, but it often changes the meaning of the verb. In most cases, these verb-preposition combinations are fixed: you could not leave the preposition out or use a different one without at least changing the meaning and probably making no sense at all.

The following selection of Spanish verbs are either linked to their object by a preposition, which may not obviously correspond to the English preposition, or in English the verb may take a direct object.

No podemos *contar con* mi hijo. *Carece de* sentido común con los regalos, pero esta vez *ha dado con* un regalo interesante.	We can't *rely on* my son. He *lacks* common sense with presents, but this time he has *hit upon* an interesting present.

(i) *Verbs linked with **a***

acercarse a	approach, get near to
asistir a	witness, be present at
contestar a	answer
jugar a	play (a game)
oler a	smell of
parecerse a	resemble
responder a	answer
saber a	taste, smack of
sobrevivir a	survive, outlive
traducir a	translate into

(ii) *Verbs linked with **con***

acertar con	hit upon, come/run across
casarse con	get married to
contar con	rely, count on; possess
cumplir con	fulfil (duty)
dar con	hit upon, come/run across
encontrarse con	meet
llenar con	fill with
soñar con	dream of

(iii) *Verbs linked with **de***

aburrirse de	get bored with
acabar de	have just
acordarse de	remember
cambiar de	change
carecer de	lack
cuidar de	take care of, look after
depender de	depend on
desconfiar de	mistrust
enamorarse de	fall in love with
enfadarse de	get annoyed at
entender de	know about
enterar de	inform about
enterarse de	find out about
equivocarse de	be wrong/mistaken about
felicitar de	congratulate on
llenar de	fill with
olvidarse de	forget

persuadir de	persuade of
preocuparse de	worry about
prescindir de	do without
reírse de	laugh at
servir de	serve as, be used for
tratar de	deal with
tratarse de	be a question of

Note **Persuadir** is followed by **a** when linked to a verb and **de** when linked to a noun.

Me *persuadieron a ir* a ver al médico.	They *persuaded* me *to go* and see the doctor.
Me *persuadieron de la necesidad* de ir.	They *persuaded* me *of the need to go*.

(iv) *Verbs linked with **en***

fijarse en	notice, pay attention to
gozar de	enjoy
insistir en	insist on
quedar en	agree to, decide on
reparar en	notice

(v) *Verbs linked with **por***

entusiasmarse por	become enthusiastic about/keen on
estar por	be in favor of (something)
felicitar por	congratulate on
inquietarse por	get anxious about
interesarse por	be interested in
luchar por	struggle, fight for
optar por	choose, opt for

(vi) Conversely, the following verbs which are linked to their object by a preposition in English, take a direct object in Spanish.

aprovechar	take advantage of, benefit from
buscar	look for
escuchar	listen to
mirar	look at
pagar	pay for (when only direct object is expressed)
pedir	ask for

Mi hijo prefiere jugar con su ordenador a *mirar la televisión* **o** *escuchar la radio.*	My son prefers playing with his computer to *watching television* or *listening to the radio.*

8j   Verbs + a 'bare' infinitive

(i)   The following are the main verbs which govern a bare infinitive without any connecting preposition.

aconsejar	advise to	**oír**	hear
acordar	agree, decide to	**olvidar**	forget to
anhelar	long to	**optar**	choose, opt to
aparentar	appear, seem to	**ordenar**	order to
buscar	seek to	**osar**	dare to
confesar	confess to	**parecer**	seem, appear to
conseguir	manage to, succeed in	**pensar**	intend to
		permitir	permit, allow to
consentir	allow to	**poder**	be able to
deber	have to, must	**preferir**	prefer to
decidir	decide to	**presumir**	presume to
declarar	declare to	**pretender**	seek, endeavor to
dejar	allow to, let		
desear	want, desire to	**procurar**	try, endeavor to
determinar	determine to	**prohibir**	forbid to, prohibit
dignarse	deign to		
esperar	hope, expect to	**prometer**	promise to
evitar	avoid -ing	**proyectar**	plan to
fingirse	pretend, feign to	**querer**	want to
hacer	make to, have...done	**recordar**	remember to
		rehusar	refuse to
imaginar	imagine -ing	**resistir**	resist -ing
impedir	prevent from	**resolver**	resolve to
intentar	try to	**resultar**	turn out to
lograr	succeed in, manage to	**saber**	know how to
		sentir	be sorry to, feel -ing
mandar	order to		
merecer	deserve to	**soler**	be accustomed to, usually + verb
necesitar	need to		
negar	deny -ing	**temer**	fear to
ofrecer	offer to	**ver**	see

> *Resultó ser* un programa muy
> complejo.
>
> *It turned out to be* a very complex
> program.
>
> A mi hijo le *aconsejé explicar* el
> programa a su padre, pero éste
> no le *permitió hacerlo.*
>
> I *advised* my son *to explain* the
> program to his father, but the latter
> didn't *allow* him *to do* so.

(ii) Most of the verbs which involve getting somebody or something
to do something, as in the second and third examples above,
can also be used with a subjunctive construction [➤16b(i)].

> A mi hijo le *aconsejé que*
> *explicase* el programa a su
> padre, pero éste *no le permitió*
> *que lo hiciese.*
>
> I *advised* my son *to explain* the
> program to his father, but the latter
> didn't *allow* him *to do* so.

(iii) **Creer** (believe) and **decir** (say) are used with a bare infinitive
when the subject of both verbs is the same.

> *Cree entenderlo* ahora.
>
> He thinks he understands it now.

(iv) Verbs of perception are followed immediately by the infinitive if
the action is completed, otherwise by the gerund [➤10c(iv)].

> Le *oí preguntar* si quería una
> explicación.
>
> I *heard* him *ask* if he wanted an
> explanation.

8k Verbs + preposition + infinitive

A great many verbs can be linked to a following infinitive by a
preposition. As with the nouns in paragraph 8i, this is a fixed
pairing which cannot be altered.

The most common linking prepositions are **a** and **de**, but some
others are also used.

(i) *Verb + **a** + infinitive*

Verbs linked to an infinitive with **a** include many implying:

(A) Beginning.

comenzar a	begin to	**ponerse a**	start to,
echar(se) a	burst out -ing		set about -ing
empezar a	begin to,	**romper a**	burst out
	start -ing	**(llorar)**	(crying)

(B) Motion.

acercarse a	approach,	**mandar a**	send to
	go up to	**parar a**	stop to, stop and
acudir a	come along,	**precipitarse a**	rush to, hasten to
	turn up to	**salir a**	go/come out
apresurarse a	hasten, hurry to		to/and
bajar a	go/come down to	**sentarse a**	sit down to,
concurrir a	gather to		sit down and
correr a	run to	**subir a**	go/come up
entrar a	go in to, go in		to/and
	and, enter to	**traer a**	bring to
enviar a	send to	**venir a**	come to, come
ir a	go to, go and,		and, be coming to
	be going to	**volar a**	fly to
levantarse a	get up to	**volver a**	return to, to do
llevar a	lead to		(+ verb) again

(C) Encouraging, inviting, obliging.

animar a	encourage to	**incitar a**	incite to
convidar a	invite to	**invitar a**	invite to
empujar a	drive to	**llamar a**	call to
excitar a	excite to	**llevar a**	lead to
exhortar a	exhort, encourage to	**mover a**	move to
forzar a	force to	**obligar a**	oblige to
impeler a	impel to	**persuadir a**	persuade to

(D) The following verbs also use the linking preposition **a**.

acertar a	succeed in,	**ayudar a**	help to
	manage to	**comprometerse a**	undertake to
acostumbrarse a	to get	**dedicar a**	dedicate to
	accustomed to	**decidirse a**	decide to
aprender a	learn to	**desafiar a**	challenge to,
arriesgarse a	risk -ing		defy to
aspirar a	aspire to	**determinarse a**	determine to
atreverse a	dare to	**disponerse a**	be disposed to
autorizar a	authorize to	**enseñar a**	teach to

limitarse a	limit oneself to	**resignarse a**	resign oneself to
ofrecerse a	volunteer to	**resistirse a**	resist -ing
prepararse a	be prepared to	**resolverse a**	resolve to
quedarse	remain, stay to	**tender a**	tend to
renunciar a	give up -ing		

Por fin *persuadí* a mi marido *a escuchar* a nuestro hijo.	At last I *persuaded* my husband *to listen* to our son.
Se sentaron a estudiar el programa.	*They sat down to study* the program.
Mi marido *le invitó a explicárselo* página por página.	My husband *invited him to explain it* page by page
No se resignaba a no entenderlo.	*He was not resigning himself to not understanding it.*

(ii)   *Verb + **de** + infinitive*

Verbs linked to an infinitive with **de** include:

(A) Those which indicate the ending or stopping of an action or separation from it.

cesar de	cease -ing	**hartarse de**	have enough of, get fed up with
dejar de	leave off -ing, fail to	**librarse de**	get free from
desistir de	desist from	**parar de**	stop, cease
disuadir de	dissuade from	**saciarse de**	have one's fill of, have enough of
fatigarse de	tire of	**terminar de**	finish, cease
guardarse de	take care not to		

(B) Those where the **de** conveys literally the English *of* or *from*.

abstenerse de	abstain from	**cansarse de**	get tired of
acusar de	accuse of	**desesperar de**	despair of
arrepentirse de	repent of, be sorry for	**gloriarse de**	boast of
		jactarse de	boast of
avergonzarse de	be ashamed of	**tratarse de**	be a question of

(C) The following verbs also use the linking preposition **de**.

acabar de	have just	**desdeñarse de**	scorn to, not deign to
acordarse de	remember		
alegrarse de	be pleased to	**olvidarse de**	forget to
cuidar de	take care to	**tratar de**	try to
encargarse de	undertake to		

> Mi hijo *disuadió* a mi marido *de poner* la televisión y *se encargó de enseñarle* el progama.
>
> *Trató de explicárselo* con cuidado y *se guardó de usar* muchos términos técnicos.

> My son *dissuaded* my husband *from putting* on the television and *undertook to teach* him the program.
>
> *He tried to explain* it to him carefully and *was careful not to use* a lot of technical terms.

(iii)   Verb + **en** + infinitive

Verbs linked with **en** include the following.

complacerse en	be pleased to	**obstinarse en**	persist in, continue obstinately to
consentir en	agree to		
consistir en	consist of	**ocuparse en**	busy oneself in
convenir en	agree to	**pensar en**	think of (= be minded to)
deleitarse en	take delight in, be delighted to		
		perseverar en	persevere in
dudar en	hesitate to	**persistir en**	persist in
hacer bien en	be right to/in	**porfiar en**	persist in
hacer mal en	be wrong to/in	**quedar en**	agree to
insistir en	insist on	**tardar en**	take time to
interesarse en	be interested in	**no tardar en**	not be long in
		vacilar en	hesitate to

> Mi hijo *hizo bien en perseverar* y mi marido *quedó en tomar* otra lección al día siguiente. Ahora *se interesa en comprar* más programas, pero *insiste en aprender* éste primero.

> My son *was right to persevere* and my husband *agreed to have* another lesson the next day. Now *he is interested in buying* more programs, but *he is insisting on learning* this one first.

(iv)   Verb + **por** + infinitive

Verbs linked with **por** include:

(A) Verbs of beginning and ending *by*.

comenzar por	begin by	**terminar por**	end by, finish by
empezar por	begin by	**concluir por**	conclude by
acabar por	end by, finish by		

(B) The following verbs.

esforzarse por	struggle, strive to	**luchar por**	fight, struggle to
estar por	be in favor of	**rabiar por**	long to, be dying to
estar por (hacer)	remain to be (done)	**suspirar por**	yearn to

Mi marido *se esfuerza por aprender* estas cosas, pero a veces cree que *terminará por volverse loco*.	My husband *struggles to learn* these things, but at times he thinks he *will end up by going mad*.

(v) *Verb +* **con** *+ infinitive*

Verbs linked with **con** include:

amenazar con	threaten to
contentarse con	be content to
soñar con	dream of

Mi hijo *sueña con llenar* la casa de aparatos, pero yo *amenazo con echarle* fuera si lo hace.	My son *dreams of filling* the house with gadgets, but I *threaten to throw him out* if he does.

(vi) Note also:

(A) Verbs linked with **para**.

estar para	be about to	**servir para**	be used for

¿Para qué sirven todos estos aparatos?	*What's the use of* all these gadgets?

(B) Verbs linked with **que**, including when they have a direct object.

tener que	have to, must	**hay que**	it is necessary to

¡*Hay que ver* a mi marido! ¡*Tiene* todo este nuevo programa *que aprender*!	*You should see* my husband! *He's got* this entire new program *to learn*!

(C) The verbs of continuing, **continuar** and **seguir**, are linked to the gerund [►10c(ii)], *not* the infinitive [►8l(iii)].

8l   Verbs + the present participle or 'gerund' (➤10b)

This is a very common construction in English, but the use of the gerund in Spanish linked to other verbs is limited to the following circumstances.

(i)   Estar + gerund

The gerund is used with **estar** to form the *progressive* or *continuous* tenses [➤8d(ii), 19c(i)], usually present or imperfect, though others are possible. These correspond closely with the English progressive tenses, with the proviso that the action must be/have been actually in progress at the time referred to.

¿Qué *estás haciendo*?	What *are you doing*?
Estoy viendo un partido de fútbol.	*I'm watching* a game of soccer.
Cuando les vi, los niños *estaban viendo* la televisión.	When I saw them, the children *were watching* the television.

But the simple present tense is used because the action *is not actually in progress* at the point of reference.

Mañana *no jugamos* al fútbol.	Tomorrow *we're not playing* soccer.

(ii)   Ir/venir + gerund

Ir and **venir** are sometimes used to form the progressive tenses when a cumulative progression is indicated.

Vas aprendiendo muy rápidamente	*You're learning* very quickly
Vienes haciendo muchos progresos.	*You're making* a lot of progress (i.e. *you're coming along* nicely).

(iii)   Continuar/seguir + gerund

Verbs of continuing (**continuar** and **seguir**) are *always* followed by the gerund, *never* the infinitive.

Siguieron viendo la televisión.	They *kept on watching* the television.

[For the use of the gerund standing on its own (= by/while doing), see paragraph 10c(i). For other translations of the English '-ing' ending see paragraph 10c(vi).]

8m Verbs + the past participle

The main verbs which combine with the past participle are **haber**, used for the special auxiliary in the compound past tenses [➤18c(viii)], and **ser** and **estar** (be) to form the *true* and *descriptive* passive respectively [➤17b, c].

(i) Haber + past participle

In Spanish, in contrast to French, only the one auxiliary verb is used to make up the compound past tenses, and the past participle remains unchanged: it does not have to *agree* with anything.

Han pasado toda la tarde delante del televisor.	*They have spent* all day in front of the television.
Ya habían pasado la mañana jugando al fútbol.	*They had* already *spent* the morning playing soccer.

(ii) Ser, estar and other verbs + past participle

When the past participle is used with **ser, estar** or any verb other than **haber**, it agrees in gender and number with the subject of the verb.

Los documentos *fueron escritos* empleando la nueva máquina.	The documents *were written* using the new machine.
Ya *están escritos* todos.	They *are* now all *written*.

(iii) Quedar/tener + past participle

The past participle can also be used in this way with **quedar** (remain, become) and **tener** (have).

Quedamos asombrados por la velocidad de la nueva máquina.	We *were amazed* by the speed of the new machine.

(iv)   Note the difference between the following.

He escrito los documentos.	I *have written* the documents. (perfect tense)
Tengo los documentos *escritos.*	I *have* the documents *written* (i.e. here before me).
Hice escribir los documentos.	I *had* the documents *written* (i.e. somebody else did it at my request or behest).

In the last case you use **hacer** + infinitive [➤9b(v)].

Attitudes to action: modal verbs

9a The function of modal verbs

A modal verb says something about the relationship between the subject and the full verb, which is in the infinitive [▶10a].

These are the main relationships expressed by modal verbs.

Note Object pronouns may precede the modal verb or be attached to the end of the infinitive [▶23b(ii)].

Lo quiero hacer / Quiero hacer*lo*.	I want to do *it*.
Se los queremos mandar / Queremos mandár*selos*.	We want to send *them to him*.

9b The verbs and their meanings

(i) Poder be able to, can

(A) Poder expresses in Spanish the physical or circumstantial ability to do something, and in most cases translates the English *be able, can, could*.

No *podemos* ir al concierto el sábado que viene puesto que estaremos en Sevilla.	We *cannot* go to the concert next Saturday since we shall be in Seville.
¿Puede decirnos si va a haber otros conciertos?	*Can* you tell us if there are going to be other concerts?

Care is needed when conveying the English 'could', which may be a past tense or a conditional [▶14d]. It is often helpful to rephrase the English using 'be able'.

Queríamos ir al concierto, pero *no podíamos* (*pudimos*).	We wanted to go to the concert, but we *couldn't* (= we *weren't able*).

| Aunque quisiéramos ir al concierto *no podríamos (pudiéramos)* . | Even if we wanted to go to the concert, we *couldn't* (= we *wouldn't be able*). |

(B) *Could have done* may be rendered in two ways:

• Imperfect or conditional of **poder** + **haber** + past participle, i.e. the identical construction as in English.

| *Podíamos (Podríamos) haber ido* al concierto. | We *could have gone* to the concert. |

This way tends to imply that we *were in a position to have gone,* but did not go.

• Conditional perfect [➤14e] of **poder** + infinitive.

| *Habríamos (hubiéramos) podido ir* al concierto. | We *could have gone/would have been able to go* to the concert. |

This puts less emphasis on the fact that, for whatever reason, we didn't get there.

Note This is a list of the tenses of **poder**.

Podemos ir	*Present indicative*	We can/are able to go
Podíamos ir	*Imperfect indicative*	We could/were able to go (circumstances were allowing)
Pudimos ir	*Preterite*	We could/were able to go (on a particular occasion)
Hemos podido ir	*Perfect*	We have been able to go
Podremos ir	*Future*	We shall be able to go
Podríamos ir	*Conditional*	We could/would be able to go
Podíamos haber ido	*Imperfect + perfect infinitive*	We could have gone
Podríamos/ pudiéramos haber ido	*Conditional* or **-ra** *imperfect subjunctive + perfect infinitive*	We could have gone
Habríamos/ hubiéramos podido ir	*Conditional* or **-ra** *imperfect subjunctive + past participle*	We could have gone/ would have been able to go

(C) To indicate an acquired skill or know-how, use **saber**.

Me gusta escuchar la música pero *no sé* leerla. *No puedo* ir a los conciertos porque donde vivo no hay autobuses y *no sé* conducir.	I like listening to music, but I *can't* (*don't know how to*) read it. I *can't* (circumstances don't allow me to) go to concerts because where I live there are no buses and I *can't* (*don't know how to*) drive.

(D) *Can* is often not expressed in Spanish with verbs of perception.

¿*Ves* el anuncio del concierto? –No, *no lo encuentro* en ninguna parte.	*Can you see* the concert ad? –No, I *can't find* it anywhere.

(E) To express permission and possibility, *can* is often loosely used in English, where *may* would be more correct. For phrases such as *may I?* and other uses of *may* see paragraph **F** below.

• The most common way of asking and granting permission to do something is to use **poder** + infinitive.

¿*Puedo* acompañarte al concierto? –¡Claro que *puedes!*	*May I* accompany you to the concert? –Of course *you may!*

• A more formal and possibly emphatic way of expressing permission is to use **permitir** with the infinitive [➤8j(i)].

No se permite fumar en los conciertos.	You *may not* smoke (you *are not allowed* to smoke) at concerts.

• The impersonal phrase [➤17e(i)] ¿**se puede?** is very commonly used when seeking permission, particularly when the action (the infinitive) is not expressed.

¿*Se puede?* ¿*Se puede* pasar? –¡No, *no se puede!*	*May I/may we?* *May I/we* come in? –No, you *may not!*

(F) *May* and *might* also express possibility. In this case, the most frequent construction in Spanish is to use **puede que** or **es posible que** + subjunctive [➤16b(v)].

| Si no vamos a Sevilla, *puede que vayamos* al concierto. | If we don't go to Seville, *we may go* to the concert. |
| Si no hubiésemos ido a Sevilla, *es posible que hubiéramos* ido al concierto. | If we had not gone to Seville, we *might have gone* to the concert. |

(ii)   Tener que, deber, hay que, haber de *must, have to*

There are several verbs in Spanish which express the idea of obligation, compulsion, of having to do something. There is considerable overlap in their respective nuances but:

(A) Tener que + infinitive suggests obligation because of circumstances.

| No fuimos al concierto porque *tuvimos que ir* a una reunión aquel día. | We didn't go to the concert because *we had to go* to a meeting that day. |

(B) Hay que + infinitive is an impersonal verb [➤8h(iii), 8k(vi)] meaning *it is necessary to*, which therefore puts more emphasis on the need for the action than on a particular doer. Unlike *il faut* in French it can only be used with the infinitive, never with the subjunctive.

| Para conocer bien la música clásica *hay que* comprar muchos discos compactos. | To get to know classical music well *one needs/you need* to buy a lot of compact discs. |

(C) Deber, which as a noun means *duty*, implies moral obligation.

| *Debemos ir* a Sevilla a ver al tío enfermo. | We must go (as a duty) to Seville to see our sick uncle. |

➤   See also 9b(ii)**F** below.

(D) Deber de + infinitive implies supposition.

| *Debe de ser* un concierto muy interesante. | *It must be* a very interesting concert. |
| *Deben de haber ido* al concierto sin nosotros. | *They must have gone* to the concert without us. |

(E) Haber de is less frequently used, but suggests *what is to happen*.

El sábado que viene *hemos de ir* a Sevilla.	Next Saturday *we are to go* to Seville.

(F) Deber also means *ought, should*. *Ought* and *should* in English express moral obligation to do something. In Spanish you normally use the conditional of **deber** + infinitive (although sometimes the present tense can have the meaning *ought* [➤9b(ii)C].

Deberíamos (debemos) ir al concierto.	We *ought to/should go* to the concert.

(G) There are two ways of saying what *ought to have/should have* happened.

• Imperfect or conditional of **deber** + **haber** + past participle, which is very close to the English construction.

Debíamos (deberíamos) haber ido al concierto.	We *ought to have gone* to the concert.

• Conditional perfect [➤14e] or **-ra** imperfect subjunctive [➤18c(vii)] of **deber** + infinitive.

Habríamos (hubiéramos) debido ir al concierto.	We *ought to/should have gone* to the concert.

Note There is a wide variety of nuances in the use of **deber**, but the following list of tenses and their equivalents should prove helpful.

Debemos ir	*Present indicative*	We must go, we should go
Debíamos ir	*Imperfect indicative*	We had to go (circumstance)
Debimos ir	*Preterite*	We had to go (at that moment)
Hemos debido ir	*Perfect*	We have had to go/we must have gone
Deberíamos ir	*Conditional*	We ought to go
Debiéramos ir	*-ra imperfect subjunctive*	We ought to go
Deberemos ir	*Future*	We shall have to go
Debíamos haber ido	*Imperfect + perfect infinitive*	We ought to/should have gone

Deberíamos haber ido	*Conditional + perfect infinitive*	We ought to/should have gone
Habríamos/ hubiéramos debido ir	*Conditional or -ra imperfect subjunctive + past participle*	We ought to/should have gone

(iii) **Querer, desear** *want to, would like to*

(A) The most common way of saying you want to do something is the verb **querer** + the infinitive.

Queremos ir al concierto pero no podemos.	*We want to go to the concert but we can't.*

A slightly more formal verb is **desear**, used in the same way.

Pues, ¿qué *desea hacer*?	*Well, what do you wish to do?*

(B) Querer is also used to translate *will* in the sense of *be willing to*.

¿*Quiere decirme* a qué hora empieza el concierto?	*Will you tell me what time the concert starts?*

(C) To say you *would like* to do something, the usual way is to use the **-ra** imperfect subjunctive form of **querer**, i.e. **quisiera** + the infinitive.

Quisiéramos ir al concierto.	*We would like to go to the concert.*

You can also use the conditional [➤14d] of **gustar**.

Nos gustaría ir al concierto.	*We would like to go to the concert.*

(D) To say you would like to have done something, use the conditional perfect [➤14e] of either verb.

Hubiéramos querido/nos hubiera gustado ir al concierto.	*We would have liked to have gone to the concert.*

⚠ When you want or would like someone else to do something, you must use **querer** or **gustar** + **que** + the subjunctive [➤16b(i)].

Quisiéramos que Vds fueran al concierto en nuestro lugar.	*We would like you to go to the* concert instead of us.

(iv)   *Ir a*   *be going to*

To say what you are or were going to do, use **ir a** + infinitive.

➤ There is more about the future tense in sections 14a, b and c.

(v)   *Hacer*   *getting or having things done*

To say you are having or getting something done, you use **hacer** followed *immediately* by the infinitive.

Cuando decidimos ir al concierto, *hicimos reservar* las entradas.	When we decided to go to the concert, we *had* tickets *reserved*.

(vi)   *Some other common verbs used as modals*

acabar de	have just
soler	be accustomed to, usually (do)
volver a	do again

Acabo de cancelar una cita. No *suelo hacer* tales cosas, y no *volveré a hacerlo*.	*I've just cancelled* an appointment, I don't *usually do* such things, and I *won't do it again*.

10 Verb forms not related to time: non-finite forms

10a The infinitive

The infinitive is the part of the verb most commonly listed in dictionaries. It names a certain activity or state without saying when it happens. It often completes the meaning of the main verb.

(i) Infinitive endings

In Spanish, the infinitive will end in **-ar** (**hablar**)
-er (**beber**)
or **-ir** (**subir**).

(ii) Uses of the infinitive

The main uses of the infinitive are described in these paragraphs:

➤
- 8j 'bare' infinitives;
- 8k verbs + prepositions + infinitives;
- 9b modal verbs + infinitives.

(iii) The infinitive as a noun

Because it is a name, an infinitive often functions like a noun or may even be made into one, often corresponding to the English verb form '-ing'. Sometimes the masculine definite article is used with it.

(El) fumar **40 cigarrillos al día le va a causar daño.**	*Smoking* 40 cigarettes a day is going to do him harm.

(iv) Prepositions + infinitive

The infinitive is the only part of the verb that can be used after prepositions [➤25d]. In addition to those which link a preceding verb to the infinitive, it is often used with the following.

antes de	before	**para**	(in order) to
después de	after	**sin**	without
en lugar de	instead of	**en vez de**	instead of

Mi hermano fuma *sin parar*. *En lugar de dejar* de fumar, busca razones *para defender* su hábito. Debería pensar *antes de seguir* fumando.	My brother smokes *without stopping*. *Instead of giving up* smoking, he looks for reasons *to defend* his habit. He ought to think *before going on* smoking.

(v) The infinitive is often used after certain prepositions [➤25] to replace a clause beginning with a conjunction. The infinitive can have a different subject from that of the main verb.

(A) Al + the infinitive is the equivalent of 'on ...ing', or a time clause beginning with **cuando** (when) [➤5a(ii), 16c(i), 26d].

Al hablarle (cuando le habló) *el médico* sobre este asunto, mi hermano no estaba contento. *Al volver* (cuando volvió) del médico estaba inquieto.	*When the doctor spoke to him about this matter*, my brother wasn't very happy. *When he got back* from the doctor's, he was uneasy.

(B) A , or more commonly, **de** + the infinitive is the equivalent of **si** (if) + a clause of condition [➤16h].

De/a ser verdad (si es verdad) lo que dijo, va a tener problemas. *De/a haber sido verdad* (si hubiera sido verdad), hubiera tenido problemas.	*If* what he said *is true*, he is going to have problems. *If it had been true*, he would have had problems.

(C) Con + the infinitive is the equivalent of a clause beginning with **aunque** (although) [➤16c(iii)] or **si** (if) [➤16h].

Con ser (aunque era) muy grave el asunto, no se preocupaba demasiado. *Con fumar* (si fumara) un poco menos, solucionaría el problema.	*Although* the matter *was* very serious, he was not that worried. *If he smoked* a little less, he would solve the problem.

(D) Por + the infinitive is the equivalent of **porque** + a clause of reason [➤5a(ii), 26d].

***Por ser** (porque era)* **tan grave el asunto, tuvimos que convencerle.**	*Because* the matter was so serious, we had to convince him.

(vi)   The infinitive is sometimes used as an imperative [➤15c(i)].

10b   *What is the present participle or gerund?*

Most Spanish grammars refer to the part of the verb that ends in **-ando** or **-iendo** as **el gerundio** (the gerund), because its form derives from the gerund in Latin. The Spanish gerund differs from what we call the *present participle* in English and French, in so far as it cannot be used as an adjective, as in *running water* or *eau courante*, though its other uses correspond to those of English and French. To be consistent, should you consult other Spanish grammars, we have referred to this part of speech throughout this book as the gerund. Readers should not, however, confuse this part with the verbal noun, as in '*Smoking* is bad for you', which is called the gerund in English!

10c   *Main uses and non-uses of the gerund*
(i)   *By doing, while doing, because of doing*

The gerund has a verbal function and usually means *by doing*, *while doing* or *because of doing*.

***Fumando** tantos cigarrillos al día se va a matar.*	*By smoking* so many cigarettes a day, he's going to kill himself.
***Viajando** por Sudamérica vimos cuánta gente fuma.*	*While (by) travelling* around South America we saw how many people smoke.
Le dije eso, *sabiendo* **que le gustaría.**	I told him that, *(while) knowing* it would please him.
***Siendo** terco, no ha podido dejar la costumbre.*	*Being (because he is)* stubborn, he has not been able to kick the habit.

(ii)   *Progressive tenses and continuing*

It is also used after **estar**, and sometimes **ir** and **venir** to form the *progressive* tenses [➤19c(i)] and after verbs of continuing [➤8k(vi)].

Mis compañeros *están viajando* por Sudamérica.	My companions *are travelling* around South America.
Siguen haciendo muchos amigos.	*They are continuing to make* lots of friends.

(iii)   *Llevar* + gerund

It can also be used with **llevar** (carry) to indicate *since when* the action has or had been going on [➤12a(iv), 13b(v)].

Llevamos (llevábamos) dos semanas trabajando sobre el asunto.	We have (had) been working on the matter for two weeks.

(iv)   *Ongoing action*

It is used to denote the ongoing action of an object of verbs of perception, representation, discovery, etc.

A los niños les pillé fumando.	I caught the children smoking.
Te vi hablando con mi hermano.	I saw you (while you were) talking to my brother.

Note   The use of the infinitive would imply that the action, i.e. the conversation, was completed.

Te vi hablar con mi hermano.	I saw you talk to my brother (i.e. and then walk away).

(v)   *-ing: adjectival forms*

With the exception of the phrase **agua hirviendo** (boiling water), this part of the verb is *never* used as an adjective, and its form never changes to agree with anything. If you wish to say *running water*, *a charming city*, *a travelling circus*, there is *usually*, but not necessarily, one of two possible adjectival forms derived from the infinitive:

-ante from **-ar** verbs, **-iente** from **-er** and **-ir** verbs

volar	**volante**	flying
crecer	**creciente**	growing

-ador from **-ar**, **-edor** from **-er** and **-idor** from **-ir** verbs

encantar   encantador   charming

Note that the latter form has a feminine adjectival form.

Es una ciudad *interesante y encantadora*, que tiene una población *creciente*.	It's an *interesting and charming* city, which has a *growing* population.

 It is not possible to predict which form a verb will use, or indeed if any particular verb has such a form; you will need to refer to a dictionary. If there is no such form, use a relative clause [➤23k] or an adjective in its own right.

Enséñeme un *modelo que funcione* de su *bicicleta plegable*.	Show me a *working model* of your *folding bicycle*.

(vi)   *-ing* elsewhere

In other circumstances, the English verb ending '-ing' is usually rendered by the infinitive in Spanish, either dependent upon another verb (with or without a linking preposition [➤8j, k]) or used as a verbal noun [➤10a(iii)]. If the subjects of the two verbs are different, a subjunctive may be needed [➤16b(i)].

¡Deja de *hacer* eso!	Stop *doing* that!
Siempre insistes en *fumar*.	You always insist on *smoking*.
Te va a matar tanto *fumar*.	So much *smoking* is going to kill you.
Pero me gusta *fumar*, no me gusta *comer* caramelos.	But I like *smoking*, I don't like *eating* sweets.
De todos modos, no me gusta que *fumes* tanto.	Anyway, I don't *like* you smoking so much.
Antes de *entrar*, ¡apaga tu cigarillo!	Before *coming in*, put your cigarette out!

10d   The past participle

The main uses of the past participle are as follows.

(i)   *Compound past tenses*

To form the compound past tenses (perfect, pluperfect, future perfect, conditional perfect, past anterior) with the auxiliary verb **haber** [▶19f].

Han llegado temprano.	*They have arrived* early.
Habrán terminado el trabajo.	*They will have finished* work.

Note   Used in this way, the past participle never changes its ending.

(ii)   *Passive with **ser/estar***

To form the passive [▶17b, c] with **ser** or **estar**. In this case, the past participle agrees in gender and number with the subject of **ser** or **estar**.

Los documentos *fueron mandados* al jefe.	The documents *were sent* to the boss.

(iii)   *Adjective*

As an adjective, with normal adjectival gender and number agreement [▶22a(i)]. It is often used with **estar**, **parecer**, etc., indicating a state [▶17c].

estos documentos *escritos*	these *written* documents
Los documentos *están escritos* en español.	The documents *are written* in Spanish.
El jefe *está (parece) muy cansado* hoy.	The boss *is (seems) very tired* today.

• Some past participles have become an adjective in their own right and may be used with **ser** with no hint of a passive.

***Somos aficionados* a la música.**	*We're* music *fans/keen on* music.

(iv)   *Noun*

Occasionally as a noun, seldom translatable by one word in English.

***los desaparecidos* de la guerra sucia**	the *'disappeared'* (those who disappeared) in the dirty war

los *desterrados*	those *in exile* (the exiled ones)

(v) *Participle clauses*

In *participle* clauses, where English may need a relative or other construction.

Franco, *muerto* en 1975, fue dictador durante casi 40 años.	Franco, *who died* in 1975 (*died* 1975), was dictator for nearly 40 years.

Quite frequently in formal written style the past participle is used in absolute clauses meaning *something having been done* or *when something has/had been done*.

***Restaurada* la línea telefónica pudieron continuar las discusiones.**	*When the telephone line had been restored* (*the telephone line having been restored*), they were able to continue the discussions.

⑪ The passage of time and the use of tenses

11a   What do tenses tell us?

Tense is not the same thing as *time*, though the same words are often used to refer to both. Time is a fact of life, in which there are only three time zones (past, present and future). Tenses, on the other hand, are grammatical structures which often reflect a way of looking at an event as well as recording when it happened. Both the number of tenses, the names given to them and their uses vary greatly from one language to another.

11b   One word or two? Simple and compound tenses

In the language of grammar, a *simple* tense is a one-word form, while a *compound* tense uses two or more words (an auxiliary verb + the past participle or gerund, depending on the tense).

Spanish verbs have two series of tenses: the *simple* and the *progressive* (or *continuous*). We refer to the latter type as *progressive* tenses throughout this book. Theoretically any tense can have a progressive form, though they are most frequently used in the present and imperfect.

¿Qué *estabas haciendo* cuando te vimos? –*Estaba comprando* un disco compacto.	What *were you doing* when we saw you? –*I was buying* a compact disc.

11c   Auxiliary verbs used to form compound tenses

(A) All the compound past tenses – perfect, pluperfect, future perfect, conditional perfect and past anterior – are formed with the auxiliary verb **haber** + the past participle. In these tenses there is no agreement of the past participle, and no pronoun or any other word may be placed between the auxiliary verb and the past participle (except on the end of the infinitive **haber**).

> ¿Lo *ha terminado* Vd ya? ¡Qué
> bien *haberlo terminado!*
>
> *Have* you *finished* it already? How
> nice *to have finished it!*

(B) The progressive tenses are formed with **estar** (and sometimes **ir** or **venir**) + the gerund [➤10b, c]. The most commonly
used are the present and imperfect progressive [➤19c(i)],
although it is possible to make up a progressive form of almost
any tense.

> ¿Qué *habrías estado haciendo*
> ahora?
>
> What *would you have been doing*
> now?

The example is the progressive form of the conditional perfect.

(C) The true passive, i.e. the form which describes the action
which *is/was/will be/* etc. *done,* is formed with the relevant
tense of **ser** [➤8d(i), 17b].

> El coche *fue aparcado* en la
> plaza por su dueño.
>
> The car *was parked* in the square
> by its owner.

 Estar is also used with the past participle [➤10d] to indicate a state
resulting from an action. This is sometimes called the descriptive passive. It is not really a compound tense, but be careful to distinguish
between the uses of **ser** and **estar** + the past participle [➤17b, c].

> El coche *estaba aparcado* en la
> plaza cuando lo remolcó la
> grúa.
>
> The car *was parked* in the square
> when the crane towed it away.

(i.e. It was in the *parked state* in which its owner had left it.)

(D) Ir a (be going to) and **acabar de** (have just) are auxiliary
verbs which are also used to give a time context to a sentence
[➤9b(iv), (vi)].

11d   *Which tense follows which?*

There is usually little problem for the English speaker in choos-
ing the most suitable Spanish tense, as in many cases the
tenses correspond exactly. Care should be taken, however,
with the following:

• when converting direct to indirect speech [➤5c];

• in time clauses involving the subjunctive [➤16c(i)];

• with the sequence of tenses when using the subjunctive [➤16g];

• in the rather more limited use of progressive tenses in Spanish than in English [➤12b].

⟨12⟩ **The present tenses**

Note The *indicative* tenses explained in chapters 12 to 14 (as opposed to *subjunctive* tenses explained in chapter 16), are used to assert that something is true or certain.

12a   The simple present [➤18c(i)]

This has a variety of functions. It can describe the following.

(i)   What the situation is now

¿Qué *haces* ahí? –Me *afeito*.	What *are you doing* there? –I'm *shaving*.

See also the present progressive [➤12b].

*(ii)   What happens **sometimes** or **usually***

Los domingos *me levanto* tarde.	On Sundays I *get up* late.

Note The auxiliary verb **soler** [➤9b(vi)] is sometimes used to say what you are *accustomed to do* or *usually do*.

***Suelo afeitarme* por la mañana.**	*I usually shave* in the morning.

(iii)   What is going to happen soon

¡*Nos vamos* en diez minutos! **– Vale, ya *voy*!**	*We're leaving* in ten minutes. – All right, *I'm coming*!

*(iv)   What has been happening **up to now** and may be going to continue*

There are two ways of expressing this with the simple present – **¡Hace horas que te *espero*!** or **¡Te *espero* desde hace horas!**

Note There is another very common construction used to express what has been happening *up to now*, using **llevar** (carry) + the gerund [➤10c(iii)].

¡*Llevo* horas *esperándo*te!	*I've been waiting* for you for hours!

(v) *Narrative present*

Events in the (usually recent) past that the speaker wishes to bring to life. This is called the *historic* or *narrative* present. It is used rather more frequently in Spanish than in English.

Te *llamo* – y ¿qué *veo*? – ¡todavía *estás* en la cama!	I *call(ed)* you – and what *do (did)* I *see?* – you *are (were)* still in bed!

12b   The present progressive [➤*19c(i)*]

The present progressive is formed with the present tense of **estar** + the gerund [➤8d(ii), 19c(i)]. In some circumstances it may also be formed using **ir** or **venir** as the auxiliary.

It is used as an alternative to the simple present [➤12a(i)] but the action *must* be in progress at the time referred to.

¿Qué *estás haciendo* ahí? –Me *estoy afeitando.*	What *are you doing* here? –*I'm shaving.*

 You cannot use this tense to say what *is happening shortly*, as in 12a(iii).

 The past tenses

Spanish has the following past tenses: the preterite, the imperfect, the perfect, the pluperfect and the past anterior.

13a   *The simple past or preterite [▶19b]*

(i)   Single, completed actions

The preterite, also sometimes referred to as the simple past or the past historic tense, is used mainly when recounting single, completed actions in the past. It tells you what *happened* on a particular occasion.

El año pasado *pasé* mis vacaciones en Méjico. *Viajé* en avión.	Last year I *spent* my vacation in Mexico. I *travelled* by plane.
Visité varios monumentos aztecas.	I *visited* several Aztec monuments.

(ii)   Completed time period

It also sums up a completed period of time, even though this may have lasted weeks or even centuries.

Fueron unas vacaciones estupendas.	*It was* a superb vacation.
A mi parecer la civilización azteca *fue* muy extraña.	In my opinion the Aztec civilization *was* a very strange one.

13b   *The imperfect [▶19b]*

The imperfect is used to refer to an action in the past, of which the beginning or end is of no relevance to the context. In practice, therefore, it is used in the following situations.

(i)   To describe what was going on at the time of reference

En la capital todavía *reconstruían* los barrios destruidos en el terremoto.	In the capital they *were* still *rebuilding* the districts destroyed in the earthquake.

Note   There is also a progressive form of the imperfect which may be used in these circumstances [➤19c(i)].

En la capital todavía *estaban reconstruyendo* los barrios destruidos en el terremoto.	In the capital they *were* still *rebuilding* the districts destroyed in the earthquake.

(ii)   To give a descriptive background in the past

Había mucha gente alrededor de la catedral, y aunque *hacía* calor y *brillaba* el sol, una nube de humo *colgaba* encima de la ciudad.	There *were* a lot of people around the cathedral, and although it *was* hot and the sun *was shining*, a cloud of smoke *hung* over the city.

(iii)   *used to*

It is used to describe repeated or habitual actions in the past, often conveying the idea of *used to*. In this use it is often accompanied by adverbs or adverbial phrases of time indicating repetition, such as **a menudo** (often), **a veces** (sometimes) [➤27b].

Cuando *vivía* en el Reino Unido *iba* a menudo a España.	When I *lived (used to live)* in the United Kingdom I often *went (used to go)* to Spain.

 The English simple past does not distinguish between *completed* single actions (or a completed series of them) and repeated actions or description. Compare the following sentences.

Viví seis años en el Reino Unido antes de ir a los Estados Unidos.	I *lived* in the United Kingdom for six years before going to the USA.

(The action of living six years is completed, the verb **vivir** is therefore in the preterite.)

> **Mientras *vivía* en el Reino Unido *visité* España tres veces.**
>
> While *I was living* in the UK, I *visited* Spain three times.

(The action of living is incomplete and descriptive, therefore in the imperfect; the action of visiting – a complete series of three visits – is therefore in the preterite.)

> **Cuando *vivía* en el Reino Unido *iba* a España todos los años.**
>
> When I lived (*used to live/was living*) in the UK, I went (*used to go*) to Spain every year.

(Both actions are repeated, with no reference to their beginning or end, therefore both verbs are in the imperfect.)

The modal **soler** (be accustomed to) is often used in the imperfect to describe what you *used to do*.

> **Cuando vivía en el Reino Unido *solía ir* a España todos los años.**
>
> When I lived in the UK, I *used to go* to Spain every year.

 Note also the contrast between a progressive background action in the imperfect or imperfect progressive and *one-off* events in the preterite.

> **¡Pensar que yo *me divertía* (*me estaba divirtiendo*) en Méjico cuando usted tuvo que volver al trabajo! ¡Y que *tomaba* (*estaba tomando*) una cerveza al lado de la piscina cuando me *llamó* por teléfono!**
>
> To think that I *was enjoying myself* in Mexico when you *had to* go back to work! And that I *was having* a beer beside the pool when you *phoned* me!

(iv) Instead of conditional [➤14d(i), 16h(ii)]

In spoken Spanish, the imperfect is sometimes used instead of the conditional.

> **Si tuviera la oportunidad de ir a Sudamérica, ¡claro que la *tomaba*!**
>
> If I had the opportunity to go to South America, of course I *would take* it!

(v) *Desde hace, llevar*

When something *had been going on* a certain time, and might well have continued, the construction with **desde hace** [➤12a(iv)] is used, with both the verb and **hacía** in the imperfect. The construction with **llevar** [➤10c(iii)]) is also commonly used.

Hacía seis años que vivía en el Reino Unido, cuando me fui a los Estados Unidos. *Vivía desde hacía seis años* en el Reino Unido, cuando me fui a los Estados Unidos. *Llevaba seis años viviendo* en el Reino Unido, cuando me fui a los Estados Unidos.	*I had been living* in the UK for six years, when I went off to the USA.

13c *The perfect [➤19c(ii)]*

The perfect, sometimes called the *present perfect*, is a compound tense made up of the auxiliary verb **haber** and the past participle. As such, it corresponds almost exactly to the English perfect tense. It is used to indicate what *has happened* in the recent past *up to now*.

¿Han visitado ustedes Méjico? –No, *no hemos visitado* Méjico, pero *hemos estado* dos veces en Guatemala.	*Have you visited* Mexico? –No, *we haven't visited* Mexico, but *we've been* to Guatemala twice.

It *may* be used in place of the preterite [➤13a] to indicate a single event in the very recent past, but this use is nowhere near as widespread as the use of the perfect as the 'one-off' past in French.

¿Han visto Vds la catedral? –Sí, la *hemos visto* esta mañana.	*Have you seen/did you see* the cathedral? –Yes, *we've seen it/we saw* it this morning.

 It is perfectly possible to have a perfect progressive [➤19c(i)] if the duration of the action needs to be emphasized.

> ¿Qué *han estado haciendo* esta mañana? *–Hemos estado visitando* la catedral.
>
> What *have you been doing* this morning? *–We've been visiting* the cathedral.

However, if 'since when' is indicated, the *present tense*, not the perfect must be used with **hace...que**, **desde hace** or **llevar** [▶12a(iv)].

13d   *The pluperfect [19c(ii)]*

This is a compound tense formed with the imperfect of the auxiliary **haber** and the past participle. It corresponds in most cases to the English pluperfect, indicating what *had happened before* a subsequent event in the past. Its name means *more than perfect, further back in the past*.

> Antes de ir a Méjico, ya *habíamos visitado* Guatemala dos veces.
> Ah, pero no me lo *había dicho*.
>
> Before going to Mexico, we *had* already *visited* Guatemala twice.
> Ah, but you *hadn't told* me that.

 When you wish to say that something had been going on for a certain time, and was likely to continue, you use the imperfect, not the pluperfect, with **hacía...que** or **desde hacía** or the imperfect of *llevar* + the gerund [▶13b(v)].

13e   *The past anterior*

This is a compound tense formed with the preterite of the auxiliary **haber** and the past participle. It is *only* used, usually in literary style, after certain time phrases to indicate *when, as soon as,* etc. an event *had happened*.

> Cuando los españoles *hubieron conquistado* Méjico, se pusieron a convertir a los indios al cristianismo.
>
> When the Spanish *had conquered* Mexico, they set about converting the Indians to Christianity.

It occurs after the following time conjunctions when they refer to an event which *had happened* in the past. However, in speech, and often in writing, it is usually replaced by the preterite or pluperfect.

después (de) que	after	**no bien**	no sooner
así que	as soon as	**cuando**	when
luego que	as soon as	**apenas**	hardly
tan pronto como	as soon as		

Cuando los españoles *conquistaron / habían conquistado* **Méjico...**

When the Spaniards *had conquered* Mexico...

14 The future and conditional tenses

14a The simple future [➤18c(iii), 19b]

The simple future is the literal equivalent of the English future tense, i.e. it tells you what will happen at a point in the future, although it is not the only, or even necessarily the most common way of expressing this concept. It is used for the following.

(i) To state simply what *will happen*

Le *escribiremos* al volver a casa.	*We'll write* to you when we get home.

(ii) To give emphatic, often rather condescending instructions, as in English

¡*Esperarás* aquí!	*You will wait* here!

(iii) To express supposition or approximation, where English uses *must*. The question form is often used where English would use the verb *wonder* + a noun clause.

¿Qué hora *será*? *Serán* las cinco y pico.	*I wonder* what the time *is*? It *must be* just after five.

 This use is more common in Spain than in Spanish-speaking America, where **deber de** tends to be used [➤9b(ii)].

14b The future perfect [➤19c]

This is a compound tense which tells you what *will have happened*. It is used:

(i) To say what *will have happened*, often by the time something else happens.

Cuando recibamos el recado ya *se habrán marchado.* Ya le *habrán enterado* del problema.	When we get the message, they *will* already *have left.* They *will* already *have informed* you of the problem.

(ii) To indicate supposition and approximation, similarly to paragraph 14a(iii), where the English verb would usually be in the perfect.

¿Dónde *habrán ido?* ¿Se *habrán perdido?* –Lo dudo, *habrán entrado* en algún bar.	I *wonder* where they *have gone?* I *wonder* if they *have got lost?* –I doubt it, they've *probably gone* into some bar or other.

14c *Alternatives to the future*

The simple future tense is not the most frequent way of expressing future time in Spanish, especially in everyday speech, and the following methods are also frequently used.

(i) *Present tense [➤12a]*

The present tense is often used, as in English, to refer to the immediate future, especially for prearranged events.

¿Qué *hacemos* esta tarde? –Primero *vamos* a la plaza, donde *nos reunimos* con Alfonso y Rosa, y luego *tomamos* algo en la terraza de un café.	What *are we doing* this afternoon? –First *we're going* to the square, where *we're meeting* Alfonso and Rosa, and then *we're having* a drink on a café terrace.

  Spanish uses the simple present here, *never* the present progressive.

(ii) *Ir a*

Spanish also uses **ir a**, in much the same way as the English equivalent *be going to* when talking about future intentions [➤9b(iv)].

¿Qué *vamos a hacer* esta tarde? –Primero *vamos a ir* a la plaza, donde nos *vamos a reunir* con Alfonso y Rosa, y luego *vamos a tomar* algo en la terraza de un café.	What *are we going to do* this afternoon? –First *we're going to go* to the square, where *we're going to meet* Alfonso and Rosa, then *we're going to have* a drink on a café terrace.

(iii) Haber de

Especially in Spanish-speaking America, the modal verb **haber de** [➤9b(ii)] is sometimes used with a future meaning, although in Spain it implies obligation and is the equivalent of *be to*.

¿Qué *hemos de hacer*?	What *shall we do/are we to do*?

Care must be taken with English expressions such as 'Will you help me?', where the English auxiliary 'will' does not express futurity but willingness [➤9b(iii)].

¿Quiere ayudarme? –No, no quiero, ¡hágalo Vd mismo!	Will you help me? –No, I won't, do it yourself!

14d The conditional [➤18c(iv), 19b]

The conditional tells you what *would happen* and has three main uses.

(i) To say what *would happen* under certain conditions, often in conjunction with **si** (if) [➤16h(ii), (iii)].

Si tuviéramos tiempo, *iríamos* a Acapulco. ¿Qué *harían* Vds en estas circunstancias?	If we had time we *would go* to Acapulco. What *would you do* in these circumstances?

(ii) In reported speech, to put the future used in direct speech into the past [➤5c].

– Iré a verles lo más pronto posible – dijo. Dijo que *iría* a verles lo más pronto posible. Creí que *haría* eso.	"I'll go and see them as soon as possible," he said. (*Direct speech*) He said (that) he *would go and see* them as soon as possible. (*Indirect speech*) I thought (that) he *would do* that.

(iii)   To express suppositions and approximations in the past, in the same way as the future is used to express them in the present [▶14a(iii)].

¿Qué *estarían haciendo*? ¿Qué hora *sería*? *Serían* las cinco y pico.	I wonder what they *were doing*? I wonder what time it *was*? It *must have been* just after five.

14e   *The conditional perfect [▶18c(viii), 19c(ii)]*

The conditional perfect is a compound tense, which tells you what *would have happened*. It is used in the following situations.

(i)   To say what *would have happened* under certain conditions, often in conjunction with **si** (if).

Si hubiéramos tenido tiempo, *habríamos ido* a Acapulco. ¿Qué *habrían hecho* Vds en estas circunstancias?	If we had had time, we *would have gone* to Acapulco. What *would you have done* in these circumstances?

See also paragraph 16h(iii) on 'if' clauses and the subjunctive.

(ii)   To express supposition and approximation [▶14a(iii), 14d(iii)].

¿Dónde *habrían ido*? ¿Se *habrían perdido*?	I wonder where they *could have gone*? I wonder if they (*could have*) *got* lost?

Some further points about the conditional and conditional perfect:

• The **-ra** imperfect subjunctive form **hubiera**, etc. but *not* the **-se** form, is frequently used as an alternative to the conditional **habría**, especially as an auxiliary [▶14e(i), 16h(iii)].

> **Si hubiéramos tenido tiempo,**   If we had had time, we *would have*
> ***hubiéramos visitado* Acapulco.**   *visited* Acapulco.

- This also occurs with **quisiera** for **querría** (would like), **pudiera** for **podría** (could) and **debiera** for **debería** (ought, would have to). It only occurs with other verbs in literary style [➤9b].

 'Would' in English does not necessarily imply condition and may denote willingness, when the imperfect or preterite of **querer** is used [➤9b(iii)].

> **No *querían/quisieron***   They *wouldn't* help us.
> **ayudarnos.**

It may also describe habitual action in the past, when the imperfect of the verb or the modal **soler** + infinitive is used [➤9b(vi)].

> **Todos los días *tomábamos/***   Every day we *would have/used to*
> ***solíamos tomar* algo en aquella**   *have* a drink on that terrace.
> **terraza.**

15 Requests and commands: the imperative

15a What does the imperative express?

The imperative is used for a variety of purposes, including requests, commands, warnings, instructions, invitations and advice.

15b The verb used in the imperative form

(i) In Spanish, because there are four ways of saying *you* – informal singular and plural, formal singular and plural [➤23b(i)] – there are four imperative forms, both positive and negative. They all say DO something or DON'T do it!

 Remember that **usted** and **ustedes** always take the *third person* verb endings, also that *all formal* and *all negative (formal or informal)* commands use the *present subjunctive* [➤18c(ii)]. Therefore only the **tú** and **vosotros** (informal) positive commands have a non-subjunctive form [➤18d(i), 19h]

Informal

Siéntate. No te preocupes.	Sit down. Don't worry.
Tened cuidado. No os hagáis daño.	Take care. Don't hurt yourselves.

Formal

Tráigame un café. No me ponga Vd azúcar, gracias.	Bring me a coffee. Don't give me any sugar, thank you.
Quédense Vds ahí, por favor. No se levanten.	Stay there, please. Don't get up.

Note The informal plural form shown above is really only used in Spain. In Spanish-speaking America, all plural imperatives use the formal form.

(ii) The imperative may indicate:

• A request

Escríbame pronto si tiene tiempo.	*Write* to me soon if you have time.

• A command or order

¡Termine esa carta ahora mismo!	*Finish* that letter right now!

• A warning

¡No toque esa máquina!	*Don't touch* that machine!

• An instruction

Pulse toque el botón.	*Press* the button.

• An invitation

Venid a vernos.	*Come* and see us.

• A piece of advice

No lo compres.	*Don't buy* it.

15c *Other ways of expressing imperatives*

(i) *Infinitive*

The infinitive [➤10a] is sometimes used as an imperative in notices, manuals, recipes, etc., where clarity and brevity are more important than politeness.

Ver página 23.	*See* page 23.
¡No tocar!	*Don't touch!*
Cortar las patatas en trozos.	*Cut* the potatoes into slices.

(ii) *¡Que !+ present subjunctive*

The present subjunctive [▶18c(ii)] after **que** is often used to reinforce reminders and where a wish is being expressed as if after an understood verb such as **desear** or **querer** [▶16b(i)]. See also 15d below.

¡Que no olviden traer el vino!	(Mind you) *don't forget* to bring the wine!
¡Que lo pasen bien!	*Enjoy yourselves!*

(iii) *Present indicative*

In colloquial speech, the present indicative with question intonation is sometimes used to soften the command into a request. English has a similar device but usually needs to use a modal verb.

¿Me *trae* la cuenta, por favor?	*Will you bring* me the bill, please?
¿Me *dice* la hora, por favor?	*Can you tell* me the time, please?

Sometimes, also in speech, the present indicative is used with the subject pronoun [▶23b(i)].

Ustedes me siguen, por favor, y **no se pierden.**	*(You) follow me*, please, and you won't get lost.

(iv) *Future*

The future tense is used to express emphatic, often condescending instructions [▶14a(ii)].

¡Esperarás aquí!	*You will wait* here!

15d The first and third person imperatives
(i) *Let's*

There are two ways of expressing *let us (let's) do something* in Spanish.

• The rather formal way with the first person plural of the present subjunctive [▶18c(ii)].

Ahora *consideremos* este asunto.	Now *let us consider* this matter.

• The more informal and colloquial use of **vamos a** + the infinitive [▶9b(iv)]. The context or tone of voice will usually differentiate between **vamos a** = *we're going to* and **vamos a** = *let's*.

Vamos a considerarlo después de almorzar, ¿no?	*Let's consider* it after lunch, shall we?

Note, however, that in the negative, **no vamos a** is usually interpreted as meaning 'we're not going to'. 'Don't let's' is usually rendered by the present subjunctive whether the context is formal or informal.

No lo consideremos por ahora.	*Don't let's consider* it for now.

For more information on the position of object pronouns with imperative see 23b(iv).

(ii) The first person singular imperative 'Let me...!'

Let me do something is sometimes expressed by **que** + the first person singular present subjunctive.

¡Que lo haga yo!	Let me do it!

(iii) The third person imperative '(Don't) let him/her/them...!'

Similarly to (ii), to say *(don't) let him/her/them do something* you use **que** + the third person of the present subjunctive.

El Sr Ramírez está a la puerta. –Pues, ¡*que pase*!	Mr. Ramírez is at the door. –Well, *let him (come) in*!
Estoy en bata. ¡*Que no me vea* así!	I'm in my bathrobe. *Don't let him see* me like this!
¡*Que le digan* que espere!	*Let them tell him* to wait!

16 Areas of uncertainty: the subjunctive

Grammarians refer to the subjunctive as the subjunctive *mood*, and it does indeed reflect uncertainty, doubt, vagueness, negativity, unreality, etc. as the following paragraphs will illustrate. It is mainly used in subordinate clauses, in many cases beginning with **que**, but can occur in main clauses in certain forms of the imperative [➤15, 16a] and in a few other cases. It is a very important element in the Spanish language and one which will reward in-depth study. As you explore it in greater depth, you will acquire an instinct for its use.

16a *The subjunctive as imperative*

See chapter 15 above and 18c and 18d(i) for the use of the subjunctive in the various types of imperative. Note that you will have met certain subjunctive forms in common commands (**diga**, say; **oiga**, listen; **traiga**, bring) long before you study any of the other uses of the subjunctive which follow.

16b *The subjunctive in noun clauses*

These clauses act as the object (and sometimes the subject) of a verb.

(i) *Subjunctive after expressions of influence*

The subjunctive is used after verbs and noun phrases whereby the subject of the main clause gets someone or something else to perform an action. Expressions of wanting, liking, ordering, forbidding, advising, insisting, etc. come into this category.

Mi mujer *no quiere que viaje* a Sevilla en coche. *Preferiría que tomase* el avión. En todo caso *no le gusta que viaje* solo. Yo siempre *le digo que no se preocupe* y *le sugiero que invite* a su hermana a pasar unos días con ella. *Mi idea es que se ocupe* lo más posible.	My wife *doesn't want me to travel* to Seville by car. *She would prefer me to take* the plane. In any case, *she doesn't like me travelling (to travel)* alone. I always *tell her not to worry* and *suggest she invites* her sister to stay with her for a few days. *My idea is for her to keep* as busy as possible.

The most common verbs of this type are:

aconsejar que alguien + subjunctive	advise someone to
causar que	cause someone to
decir que	tell someone to
evitar que	avoid someone's -ing
gustar que (me gusta etc.)	like someone to
hacer que	make someone, cause someone to
impedir que	prevent someone -ing
insistir en que	insist on someone -ing
lograr que	bring about that
mandar que	order someone to
obligar a que	oblige someone to
pedir que	ask someone to
permitir que	permit, allow someone to
preferir que	prefer someone to
querer que	want someone to
sugerir que	suggest someone does

• Of the verbs listed above, **aconsejar**, **causar**, **hacer**, **impedir**, **mandar**, **permitir** and **sugerir** may be used with the infinitive [➤8j, 9b], even when the subject of the main verb and the infinitive would be different.

Mi mujer *no permite que yo viaje* **en coche.**	My wife *doesn't allow me to travel* by car.
Mi mujer *no me permite viajar* **en coche.**	

 Pedir (to ask, request) and **decir** (to tell someone to do something) must *always* be used with the subjunctive, unlike their equivalents in French.

Siempre *me ha pedido que viaje* **en coche.**	She *has always asked me to travel* by car.

Note   **Decir que** + *indicative* is used to say that something is happening, has happened, etc. as in reported speech [➤5c(ii)].

Mi mujer *dice* **que** *tengo* **que viajar en avión.**	My wife *says* that *I must* travel by plane.

Decir que + *subjunctive* means *to tell someone to do something*.

Mi mujer siempre me *dice* que *viaje* en avión.	My wife *is always telling* me *to travel* by plane.

 Note the difference between the English and Spanish constructions when using some of these verbs.

Ella no quiere *que yo vaya.*	*She* doesn't want *that I go* = She doesn't want *me to go.*

• Noun phrases, often but not necessarily associated with the above verbs, may also be followed by the subjunctive.

Nunca sigue mi *consejo de que invite* a su hermana, aunque *mi preferencia es que tenga* compañía cuando estoy ausente.	She never follows *my advice to invite* her sister, although *my preference is for her to have* company while I'm away.

• In the first example, the noun phrase is linked to the **que** which introduces the subjunctive by the same preposition with which it would be linked to an infinitive [➤25c].

In the second example, the noun phrase **mi preferencia es que** (my preference is that) is the equivalent of the verb **prefiero que** (I prefer that).

(ii) *Subjunctive after value judgements and emotional reactions*

The subjunctive is used after verbs and noun phrases which amount to an expression of emotional reaction or a value judgement.

Qué pena que yo tenga que viajar a Sevilla sin mi mujer.	*What a pity (that) I have to* travel to Seville without my wife.
Es natural que ella se preocupe por mí.	*It's natural that she should be worried* about me.
Es una vergüenza que mi empresa no le permita acompañarme.	*It's disgraceful that my company won't allow her* to go with me.
Pero *me alegro de que considere* invitar a su hermana.	But *I'm glad (that) she is considering* inviting her sister.

Sin embargo, *¿no sería mejor que viajara* conmigo? *Me fastidia que la empresa sea* **tan mezquina. En efecto *el que se comporte* así con sus empleados me parece mentira.**	Nevertheless, *wouldn't it be better for her to travel* with me? *It annoys me that the company is* so mean. In fact *that it should behave* like that with its employees *seems incredible* to me.

Note Plain statements of fact without an emotional reaction or value judgement, such as **es verdad que**... (it's true that) take the indicative.

Es verdad que no puede acompañarme.	It's true (that) she can't go with me.

(iii) The subjunctive is usually used after **el hecho de que**, **el que** (the fact that) and **que** (that) when its clause begins a sentence in which the main verb represents an emotional reaction or value judgement.

El hecho de que no venga **conmigo me pone triste.** *Que no venga* **conmigo me pone triste.**	*(The fact) that she's not coming* with me makes me miserable.

(iv) *Subjunctive after expressions of doubt, denial and disbelief*

It could be said that these are also emotional reactions or value judgements, but these aspects are dealt with separately, as it is important to contrast phrases of doubt, denial and disbelief, which take the subjunctive, with positive statements of certainty, which take the indicative.

Dudo que la empresa cambie **su política.** (*subjunctive*) **En efecto *estoy seguro de que no cambiará* de parecer.** (*indicative*) *No digo que no haya pensado* **en sus razones, pero *no creo que sean* muy buenas.** (*subjunctives*)	I doubt whether the company will change its policy. In fact *I'm sure it won't change* its mind. *I'm not saying that it hasn't thought* about its reasons, but *I don't think that they are* very good ones.

No cabe duda de que en otros aspectos *trata* bien a sus empleados. (*indicative*) Por eso *no creo que vaya a haber* huelgas por este asunto. (*subjunctive*)	*There is no doubt that* in other aspects *it treats* its employees well. So *I don't think there are going to be* strikes over this matter.

⚠ Expressions of doubt used negatively become expressions of certainty and take the indicative. Conversely expressions of certainty used negatively become expressions of doubt and take the subjunctive.

No estoy seguro de que la empresa *haga* bien en esto. Sin embargo, *no dudo* que *tiene* sus razones.	*I'm not sure* (that) the company *is* right in this. However, *I don't doubt* that it has its reasons.

(v) *Subjunctive after expressions of possibility and probability*

The subjunctive must always be used after the following expressions.

es posible que	it's possible that
puede (ser) que	it may be that
es probable que	it's probable, likely that
la posibilidad de que	the possibility that
la probabilidad de que	the probability, likelihood that

Hay cierta *posibilidad* de que la empresa *cambie* su política. Pero es más *probable* que *no cambie* nada.	There's a certain *possibility* that the company *might change* its policy. But it's more *likely* that it *won't change* anything.

16c *The subjunctive in adverbial clauses*

The subjunctive is used in subordinate adverbial clauses when the action *was not a reality* at the time of the action of the main verb. Some subordinating conjunctions [➤5a(ii)] will always take the subjunctive, others do sometimes, depending on the 'reality' of the action they refer to.

(i)   *Clauses of time*

The idea of reality/non-reality is probably easiest to understand in time clauses, after expressions such as *when, as soon as,* etc. Compare the following examples.

Cuando *llegue* **a Sevilla, llamaré a mi mujer.**	When I *arrive* in Seville, I'll phone my wife.

I still have to arrive before I phone, so the action is still unreal, and is therefore in the subjunctive.

Cuando *llegué* **a Sevilla, llamé a mi mujer.**	When I *arrived* in Seville, I phoned my wife.

Both verbs are facts, they both *happened*, therefore the indicative is used.

Dije que cuando *llegara/llegase* **a Sevilla, llamaría a mi mujer.**	I said that when I *arrived* in Seville, I would phone my wife.

 Although the English 'arrived' is in the simple past, in Spanish the (past) subjunctive is required, since at the time in question the action of arriving had not yet taken place.

The following conjunctions take the subjunctive when they refer to events which have or had not happened, and the indicative when the event has or had happened and is therefore a fact.

antes de que	before	**luego que**	as soon as
así que	as soon as	**mientras (que)**	while, so long as
cuando	when	**no bien**	as soon as, no
después de que	after		sooner than
en cuanto	as soon as	**tan pronto como**	as soon as
hasta que	until	**una vez que**	once

Llamé a mi mujer *mientras ella se bañaba.*	I called my wife *while she was having a bath.*
En cuanto salió del baño **me volvió a llamar.**	*As soon as she was out of the bath,* she called me back.

(ii) Clauses of purpose

The following phrases, all containing the basic idea *in order that something shall happen*, need the subjunctive since the action patently has not yet happened.

a que	in order that, so that
a fin de que	in order that, so that
para que	in order that, so that
con el objeto de que	with the object that/of

Escribí al jefe *para que* estuviese concienciado del problema.	I wrote to the boss *so that he would be aware of* the problem.
Le escribí *con el objeto de que* supiera mi parecer.	I wrote to him, *with the object that he should know/of him knowing* my opinion.

The following phrases take the subjunctive when, like those above, they mean 'in order that', but not when they mean 'with the result that' (i.e. when the action has or had clearly happened). 'So that' can have either meaning in English.

de forma que	so that	**de modo que**	so that
de manera que	so that		

Se lo dije *de forma que lo supiera*.	I told him *so that (in order that) he would know*.
Se lo he dicho varias veces, *de forma que lo sabe* muy bien.	I've told him several times, *so (with the result that) he's well aware of it*.

(iii) Clauses of concession

The subjunctive is needed after the following phrases when they refer to a hypothesis rather than a fact.

aunque	although
a pesar de que	in spite of the fact that

Voy a ver al jefe, *aunque no quiera* verme.	I'm going to see the boss *even if he doesn't want* to see me. (*Hypothesis*)
Fui a ver al jefe, *aunque no quería* verme.	I went to see the boss, although *he didn't want* to see me. (*Fact*)

• **Aunque** + the subjunctive tends to be the equivalent of the English *even if, even though*.
• **Suponiendo que** (supposing that) always takes the subjunctive because it always introduces a hypothesis.

Suponiendo que no quiera **verme...**	*Supposing he won't see me...*

(iv) Clauses of condition

The subjunctive is always used after the following conjunctions.

a condición de que	on condition that
con tal que	provided that
a menos que	unless
a no ser que	unless

A menos que me escuche **el jefe, pienso dimitir.**	*Unless the boss listens to me,* I intend to resign.
No dimitiré *a condición de que/con tal que me escuche.*	I won't resign *on condition that/provided that he listens to me.*

(v) Other conjunctions requiring the subjunctive

sin que	without
en el caso de que	in the event that/of

Escribí al jefe *sin que lo supiese* **mi mujer.**	I wrote to the boss *without my wife knowing*.
En el caso de que respondiera el jefe, **se lo diría.**	*In the event of the boss replying*, I would tell her.

(vi) Use of the infinitive when the subjects are the same

When the subjects of the main and subordinate verbs are the same, the following prepositional forms are used with the infinitive [➤10a(iv)].

al	on -ing	**hasta**	until
antes de	before -ing	**para**	in order to
a pesar de	in spite of -ing	**a fin de**	in order to
después de	after -ing	**con el objeto de**	with the object of -ing
en el caso de	in the event of -ing	**sin**	without -ing

No consulté a mi mujer *antes de* *escribirle* **al jefe.**	I didn't consult my wife *before* *writing* to the boss.

'I' is the subject of both *write* and *consult*.

Escribí la carta *con el objeto de* *darle* **un susto, lo hice** *sin* *pensar*.	I wrote the letter *with the object of* *giving* him a fright. I did it *without* *thinking*.

'I' is the subject of all four verbs: *write*, *give*, *do* and *think*.
Al + infinitive may also be used when the subjects are different [►10a(v)].

(vii) *Translating English conjunctions ending in* **-ever**

The subjunctive is used, predictably, when the statement is not a reality. In some cases the clause is introduced by a conjunction [►5a(ii)], in others the verb is *duplicated* (this is called in Spanish the **forma reduplicativa**).

(A) Cuando, siempre que whenever

Iré a ver al jefe *cuando él* *quiera*.	I'll go and see the boss *whenever* *he wishes*. (*not yet a reality*)
Siempre que *hablo* **con el jefe,** **nos disputamos.**	*Whenever I talk* to the boss, we disagree. (*a reality*)

(B) Dondequiera que, adondequiera que or *forma redu-* *plicativa* wherever

Adondequiera que viaje **prefiero** **que me acompañe mi mujer.** **}**	*Wherever I travel*, I prefer my wife to come with me.
Viaje adonde viaje, **prefiero que** **me acompañe mi mujer**	

(C) Cualquiera que whoever, anyone who

Cualquiera que crea **que nuestro** **jefe es un hombre simpático no** **le/lo conoce como yo.**	*Whoever/anyone who thinks* that our boss is a kind man doesn't know him as I do.

Similarly, to say *whoever it is*, you can use **quienquiera** or the **forma reduplicativa**.

| Yo quisiera tener un nuevo jefe, *quienquiera que fuera.* Yo quisiera tener un nuevo jefe, *fuera quien fuera.* | I'd like to have a new boss, whoever it might be. |

(D) Use the **forma reduplicativa** for *whatever*.

| *Sea cual sea el resultado*, voy a citarme con él. | *Whatever the outcome (might be)*, I'm going to make an appointment with him. |
| *Hiciera como hiciera*, no sería a mi gusto. | *Whatever he did*, it wouldn't be to my liking. |

(E) There are two ways of saying *however*: **por mucho que/por más que** + verb or **por muy** + adjective + verb.

| *Por mucho que trate* de comprenderle, me sigue pareciendo un hombre desagradable. | *However (much) I try* to understand him, he still seems an unpleasant man. |
| *Por muy desagradable que parezca*, ¡es mi jefe! | *However unpleasant he may appear*, he's my boss! |

(viii)   *Whether ... or not*

The **forma reduplicativa** of the subjunctive is also used in the following type of clause.

| Tengo que trabajar con este hombre, *quiera o no quiera.* | I have to work with this man, *whether I like it or not.* |

16d   *The subjunctive in adjectival or relative clauses [➤23k]*

(i)   *The subjunctive after the indefinite antecedent*

The subjunctive is used when the antecedent [➤23k(i)] is not exactly defined. Compare the following examples.

| Yo quisiera tener *un jefe que mostrara* más simpatía con su personal. | I'd like to have *a boss who showed* more sympathy towards his staff. |

i.e. any boss who met that condition, therefore the subordinate verb is in the subjunctive.

Mi hermano tiene *un jefe que muestra* toda la simpatía posible hacia su personal.	My brother has *a boss who shows* all possible sympathy towards his staff.

The boss is a particular, definite one, therefore the verb is in the indicative.

Si voy a Sevilla en viaje de negocios, quisiera tomar *un avión que llegase* antes de las diez.	If I go on a business trip to Seville, I'd like to catch *a plane that arrives* before ten o'clock.

i.e. any plane which arrives before ten: subjunctive.

Quisiera tomar *el avión que llega* antes de las diez.	I'd like to catch *the plane that arrives* before ten.

i.e. the (known) plane that gets there before ten: indicative.

Búsqueme *un hotel que se encuentre* algo apartado del centro y *donde pueda* descansar.	Get me *a hotel which is* a bit away from the center and *where I can* relax.

i.e. not one definite hotel: subjunctive.

Este es *un hotel que se encuentra* algo apartado del centro y *donde Vd puede* descansar.	This one is *a hotel which is* situated a bit away from the center and *where you can* relax.

i.e. a definite hotel: indicative.

• Sometimes, especially when used with **buscar**, **querer** and similar verbs, this construction also carries the idea of purpose [➤16c(ii)], and translates the English *somebody to do something*.

Busco *alguien que me encuentre* un buen hotel.	I'm looking for *someone to find me* a good hotel.

Note The personal **a** [➤8e] is needed before a definite personal direct object leading to a verb in the indicative, but not before an indefinite one leading to a verb in the subjunctive.

Necesito *un agente que me consiga* un hotel.	I need *an agent who will get/to get* me a hotel.
Necesito *a aquel agente que me consiguió* el hotel en Granada.	I need *that agent who got* me the hotel in Granada.

(ii) The subjunctive after a negative antecedent

When the existence of the antecedent is denied, the verb in the relative clause is in the subjunctive.

Parece que *no hay avión que llegue* antes de las diez.	It seems that *there isn't a plane which arrives* before ten.
No encontraba q*uien me ayudase* conseguir un buen hotel.	I couldn't find *anyone who could help me/to help me* get a good hotel.

16e The subjunctive in main clauses

In addition to the imperative uses [➤15c(ii)], the subjunctive occurs in main clauses in the following ways.

(i) ¡Ojalá!

After **ojalá**, which has its origins in Arabic and means *would to Allah!*. It expresses a strong wish that something should or should not happen. It is followed by either the present or imperfect subjunctive, the latter perhaps suggesting that the likelihood of the wish being granted is very remote.

¡Ojalá se jubile el jefe!	If only the boss would retire!
¡Ojalá me tocara la lotería!	If only I could win the lottery!

Note **Ojalá** can also stand by itself to endorse a previous statement.

Quizás el jefe se jubile dentro de poco. *¡¡Ojalá!!*	Perhaps the boss will retire soon. *I wish he would / If only!*

(ii) *After words meaning 'perhaps': **tal vez**, **quizá(s)***

Quizás *se jubile* **el año que viene.**	Maybe *he'll retire* next year.
Tal vez entonces me *hagan* **jefe.**	Perhaps they will then *make* me boss.

16f   The subjunctive in some common phrases

The following set phrases contain the verb in the subjunctive.

que yo sepa	as far as I know
que se sepa	as far as is known
que sepamos	as far as we know
o sea	in other words, to put it another way
sea como sea	be that as it may

16g   The sequence of tenses with the subjunctive

The most usual combinations of tenses are as follows.

(i)   *Main clause* in present, imperative, future, or perfect.
Subordinate clause in present or perfect subjunctive [➤18c].

Siento **que el jefe no** *quiera/no haya querido* **hablarme.**	*I'm sorry* the boss *doesn't want/didn't want (hasn't wanted)* to talk to me.
Pida Vd **al jefe que me** *escuche.*	*Ask* the boss *to listen* to me.
Bueno, le *pediré* **que te** *entreviste.*	Good, I'll ask him to *interview* you.
Le *he pedido* **que te** *vea* **mañana.**	*I have asked* him *to see* you tomorrow.

However, the imperfect subjunctive may be used with the present tense if the sense requires it.

Siento mucho **que** *no quisiera/quisiese* **hablarme.**	*I'm very sorry* (that) he *didn't want* to talk to me.

(ii)   *Main clause* in imperfect, preterite, conditional, conditional perfect, pluperfect.
Subordinate clause in imperfect or pluperfect subjunctive [➤18c].

Sentía/sentí que no **quisiera/quisiese** escucharme.	I was sorry that he didn't want to listen to me.
Sentí que no **hubiera/hubiese querido** escucharme.	I was sorry that he hadn't wanted to listen to me.
Sentiría que no me oyera.	I would be sorry if he didn't hear me.
Le **habría/hubiera dicho** que **dejase** acompañarme a mi mujer.	I would have told him to let my wife come with me.

16h 'If' clauses

➤ See also paragraph 14d on the conditional and 14e on the conditional perfect.

Whether the subjunctive is used or not in the if clause after **si** depends on the type of condition: is it open, remote, fulfilled or unfulfilled? The following are the most common structures.

(i) Open condition

The condition is entirely open, it may or may not be fulfilled: **si** is followed by the present indicative [➤18c] (never the present subjunctive), and the main verb will usually be in the present, imperative or future [➤18c], just as in English.

Si el jefe está en su despacho, **dígale** que quisiera verle.	If the boss is in his office, tell him I'd like to see him.
Si el jefe me escucha, le diré lo que pienso.	If the boss listens to me, I'll tell him what I think.

(ii) Remote condition

The condition is remote or contrary to fact: **si** is followed by either form of the imperfect subjunctive [➤18c(vii)] and the main clause is in the conditional [➤18c(iv)].

Si el jefe estuviera/estuviese le recibiría.	If the boss were in, he would receive you. (i.e. He is not/not likely to be in.)
Si él me escuchara/escuchase le explicaría mi problema.	If he listened/were to listen to me, I would explain my problem to him. (i.e. He is unlikely to listen.)

In spoken and sometimes in written Spanish, the imperfect may be used instead of the conditional in the main clause [▶13b(iv)].

Si el jefe estuviera/estuviese *me* **escuchaba.**	If the boss were in, he *would listen* to me.

(iii)   Unfulfilled condition

The condition is unfulfilled, contrary to fact: **si** is followed by the pluperfect subjunctive [▶18c(viii), 19c(ii)] (either form) and the main clause is in the conditional perfect [▶19c(ii)], where the alternative **-ra** imperfect subjunctive form of the auxiliary **hubiera** is frequently used. The simple conditional is also sometimes possible.

Si *hubiera/hubiese* **hablado con el jefe, le** *habría/hubiera dicho lo* **que pensaba.**	If I *had spoken* to the boss, I *would have told* him what I thought. (But I didn't speak to him, so I couldn't tell him anything – *condition unfulfilled*.)
Si no le *hubiese/hubiera* **molestado** tanto, *no me habría* **despedido.**	If I *hadn't pestered* him so much, he *wouldn't have fired me*. (But I *did* pester him, so he *did* fire me.)
Si *no le* **hubiese/hubiera** **molestado** tanto, todavía *tendría* **trabajo.**	If I *hadn't pestered* him so much, I *would* still *have* a job.

⚠ The use of the **-ra** form (not the **-se** form) of the imperfect subjunctive to replace the conditional is the only use where the two forms are not completely interchangeable.

(iv)   Fulfilled condition

The condition is fulfilled. In these cases *if* is often the equivalent of *when* or *because* and the most suitable tense of the indicative is used after **si**.

Si yo *quería* **hablar con el jefe, siempre él** *decía* **a su secretaria que no estaba.**	If (whenever) I *wanted* to talk to the boss, he always *told* his secretary he wasn't there.
Si *he perdido* **mi empleo, es porque mi mujer siempre quiere viajar conmigo.**	If (the reason why) I've lost my job, it's because my wife always wants to travel with me.

(v) *What if...?*

What if...? is expressed by **si** + present indicative, imperfect or pluperfect subjunctive as in the following examples.

¿*Si no consigo* otro empleo?	What if I don't get another job?
¿*Si no consiguiera* *(consiguiese)* otro empleo?	What if I didn't get another job?
¿*Si no hubiera (hubiese)* *conseguido* otro empleo?	What if I hadn't got another job?

(vi) *As if...*

As if... is expressed by **como si**, usually with the imperfect or pluperfect subjunctive.

Es *como si* lo *soñara/soñase.*	It's as if I were dreaming it.
Es *como si* lo *hubiera/hubiese* *soñado.*	It's as if I had dreamed it.

(vii) ***De/a*** + *infinitive*

De or, less commonly, **a** + the infinitive [➤10a(v)] may be used instead of **si** + a clause, when the condition is open or hypothetical and the subject of both clauses is the same.

De haber sabido que iba a despedirme, no le *hubiera molestado* tanto.	If I had known that he was going to fire me, I wouldn't have pestered him so much.
De encontrar un nuevo puesto de trabajo, *trataré* al jefe con *más* respeto.	If I find another job, I'll treat the boss with more respect.

17 Things done to you: the passive

17a What does the passive express?

In the passive, the subject is the person or thing primarily affected by the action of the verb. This is just what the direct object of a transitive verb does, and only transitive verbs can be used in the passive [▶8a(i), 8e]. All the same, the passive is not just another way of saying the same thing as the active form – it emphasizes different things, especially what happens to the subject. Who the doer is often matters less and may not be stated.

La nueva guía *será publicada* en marzo.	The new guide *will be published* in March.
Ha sido escrita por dos expertos regionales.	*It has been written by two local experts.*
Una nueva guía *es publicada* cada cinco años.	A new guide *is published* every five years.

17b Formation of the passive

The passive is formed with the relevant tense of **ser** + the past participle. Note that the past participle agrees with the subject [▶8d(i)].

La última guía *fue publicada* hace cinco años.	The last guide *was published* five years ago.
Todas nuestras guías *son traducidas* a varios idiomas por nuestros expertos.	All our guides *are translated* by our experts into several languages.

17c True versus descriptive passive

All the examples in 17a and b are of the *true* passive, which indicates the action being done to somebody or something: the last guide *was published* five years ago, i.e. the publication *happened*. In Spanish you can use **estar** [▶8d(ii), 10d(ii)] with the past participle to describe the state that somebody or something is in after the action has been done.

Todas nuestras guías *están escritas* **en varios idiomas.**	All our guides *are written* in several languages.
La nueva guía *no está publicada* **todavía.**	The new guide *is not* yet *published.* (i.e. the action of publishing it has not yet happened, therefore it is not yet in a published state)

The past participle describing a state may be found after certain other verbs, e.g. **quedar** (remain, become), **parecer** (seem, appear) [▶10d(ii)].

17d   Expressing the agent or instrument

The person or thing the action is done *by* is called the *agent* or *instrument* respectively. These would have been the subject of a transitive verb. In Spanish both the agent and instrument are introduced by **por**, meaning *by*.

La nueva guía ha sido encargada *por el director de turismo.*	The new guide has been commissioned *by the director of tourism.*
Será impresa *por una imprenta de la región.*	It will be printed *by a printing house* in the area.

• A few past participles may be encountered followed by **de**, especially when used with **estar.**

acompañado de	accompanied by
seguido de	followed by

La nueva guía *está acompañada de* **una traducción.**	The new guide *is accompanied by* a translation.

17e   Alternatives to the passive

Traditionally, the true passive with **ser** has not been anything like as popular a construction in Spanish as its equivalent in English, where it perhaps tends to be overused. However, there is evidence of its being used a lot more in recent years especially in the Spanish American press, the theory being that hurried translation of American English newsmatter is responsible!

There are, nevertheless, a number of alternative constructions which tend to be preferred.

(i) *Reflexive*

Most commonly, make the verb reflexive.

(A) The literal reflexive meaning would usually be nonsensical: *The guide will publish itself*. There is therefore no ambiguity of meaning.

Note
• If the subject is plural, the verb is also plural.
• **Por** cannot be used here to introduce an agent or instrument, i.e. you cannot express who or what the action is done by.

La nueva guía *se publicará* **dentro de poco.** *Se imprimen* **diez mil ejemplares.**	The new guide *will be published* shortly. Ten thousand copies *are being printed.*

(B) At times the **se** behaves almost like a subject pronoun [➤23b(i)], i.e. like the impersonal *one* in English or *on* in French.

Se prevé **que estas nuevas guías serán muy populares. En la oficina de turismo** *se habla inglés.*	*It is envisaged* that these new guides will be very popular. *English is spoken* in the tourist office. (c.f. 'on parle anglais')

(C) Se with a singular verb is in fact used in a range of impersonal expressions [➤23d(i)].

se cree	it is believed	**se prevé**	it is envisaged
se espera	it is hoped, expected	**se prohíbe**	it is forbidden
se dice	it is said	**se propone**	it is suggested
se permite	it is allowed, you may	**se puede**	one may
se plantea	it is proposed	**se ruega**	it is requested, you are asked

(D) This device is taken further when the subject of the verb is a person or persons and making the verb reflexive would create ambiguity.

El año pasado se nombró *al* **nuevo director de turismo.**	Last year the new director of tourism was appointed.

El año pasado se nombró el nuevo director de turismo would mean he appointed or nominated himself. **El director** is made the direct object of the verb, complete with personal **a** [▶8e], and the situation is clarified: *one appointed him.*

Note This construction is particularly useful to get over the English passive where the *indirect* object of the active verb has been made the subject of a passive verb – a construction which has no literal equivalent in Spanish: you cannot say *I was given, we were told,* etc.

Se nos dice **que las nuevas guías son muy populares.**	*We are told* that the new guides are very popular.

(E) It is also possible to maintain a similar word order to the passive construction in English and therefore to emphasize an element of the sentence in the same way [▶4g].

Al nuevo director se le nombró **el año pasado.** ***A los empleados de la oficina se les informó*** **en seguida del nombramiento.**	*The new director was appointed* last year. *The office staff were informed* at once of the appointment.

(ii) *Active*

Make the verb active. The sentence can be expressed as subject + verb + object, as in the corresponding English sentence, but this makes a completely neutral statement:

La oficina de turismo publica la guía.	The tourist office publishes the guide.

However, in Spanish the word order is flexible enough to bring out an emphasis where English has to resort to the passive. Note the need to duplicate the object with a redundant object pronoun [▶23b(v)] when the object precedes the verb and the subject follows it.

| La guía *la publica la oficina de turismo.* | The guide *is published by the tourist office.* |

(iii) *Impersonal third person plural*

If no agent is expressed, use the impersonal third person plural of the verb, *they*.

| *Nombraron* al nuevo director el año pasado. | The new director *was appointed/they appointed* the new director last year. |

 Types of Spanish verb

18a   Predictability: conjugating a verb

The whole set of a verb's stems and endings is known as its *conjugation*. The various parts of this set are predictable at several levels.

(i)   Regular verbs

Regular verbs are verbs for which you can predict any part of any tense from the spelling of the infinitive [➤10a] (plus, of course, a knowledge of the rules!). Infinitives in Spanish end in **-ar**, **-er** or **-ir**. Verbs in which some parts cannot be predicted in this way are *irregular*. Some of the commonest Spanish verbs are irregular, but if any new verb is coined, it is always conjugated on a regular pattern, usually **-ar**.

Recent imports into Spanish from other languages include the following regular **-ar** type verbs [➤19a].

dopar	dope, drug	**faxear**	fax
esnifar	sniff (solvent)	**xerocopiar**	photocopy

(ii)   Irregular verbs

Some irregular verbs form groups, so if you know one you can predict the forms of any of the others. The so-called *stem-changing* verbs in Spanish fall into this category (**pienso**, **vuelvo**, **pido**, etc.) [➤19d]; there is also a group which has a **-g-** in the first person singular of the present indicative and therefore throughout the present subjunctive (**pongo**) [➤18b(v)]; another similar group has **-zc-** in the same place (**conozco**) [➤18b(vi)]; there is also a group with the irregular **pretérito grave** [➤18b(viii)].

(iii)   Compound verbs

A compound verb is a verb where a prefix is added to the *base* verb. With very few exceptions, compound verbs [➤18e] conjugate in the same way as their base verb.

poner	put	**suponer**	suppose
pongo	I put	**supongo**	I suppose

18b   *Major groups of verbs: how are they conjugated?*

(i)   *The three major conjugations*

There are three *conjugations* or groups of verbs in Spanish, which take a set of endings according to their infinitive. The infinitive ends in **-ar**, **-er** or **-ir**. In fact, a look at the verb tables [➤19b] will show that throughout the whole range of tenses, there are only three endings in which **-er** and **-ir** verbs differ.

Infinitive	*Present indicative*	*Informal imperative plural*
com*er*	com*emos*, com*éis*	com*ed*
viv*ir*	viv*imos*, viv*ís*	viv*id*

In *all other tenses and persons* they have identical endings.

(ii)   *Stem-changing verbs [➤19d]*

The biggest group of not quite regular, but predictably irregular, verbs in Spanish are those which are variously known as *radical-changing*, *root-changing* or *stem-changing*. As elsewhere in this book we refer to the part of the verb to which endings are added as the *stem*, we will use the term *stem-changing*.

You will already probably have noticed that Spanish has many words containing the diphthong [➤2c(iii)] **-ue-** or **-ie-**, where corresponding or related words in other Latin languages or even English simply have **-o-** or **-e-**.

Spanish	*French*	*English*
puerto	po rt	po rt
muerto	mo rt	mo rtuary
siete	se pt	se ptet

This stem change often happens in Spanish when the original **-o-** or **-e-** is stressed [➤2c(i)]. When a verb is conjugated, the stress varies from stem to ending according to the person and tense, and in some verbs the stem changes according to the stress.

There are three main types of stem-changing verbs.

Type 1: **-ar** *and* **-er** *verbs*

The stem changes are: **-e-** to **-ie-**, **-o-** to **-ue-**, and **-u-** to **-ue-** (**jugar** [play] only). The changes occur only in the present indicative and subjunctive, where the stem is stressed, i.e. in all three singular forms and the third person plural.

pensar (*think*)

pienso, piensas, piensa...piensan   piense, pienses, piense...piensen

volver (*return*)

vuelvo, vuelves, vuelve...vuelven   vuelva, vuelvas, vuelva...vuelvan

jugar (*play*)

juego, juegas, juega...juegan   juegue, juegues, juegue...jueguen

Type 2: **-ir** *verbs*

Verbs of this type (e.g. **mentir** [lie]; **dormir** [sleep]) have the *same changes* in the *same places* as those of type 1, but *additionally* the stem vowel changes from **-e-** to **-i-** and **-o-** to **-u-** in:
• the gerund (**mintiendo, durmiendo**) [➤18d(ii)];
• the first and second persons plural of the present subjunctive [➤18c(ii)] (**mintamos, mintáis; durmamos, durmáis**);
• the third person singular and plural of the preterite [➤13a] (**mintió, mintieron; durmió, durmieron**);
• and therefore throughout both forms of the imperfect subjunctive [➤18c(vii)] (**mintiera/mintiese; durmiera/durmiese**).

Type 3: **-ir** *verbs*

Verbs of this type have the stem change in all the same places as type 2, but the change is *always* **-e-** to **-i-**.

pedir (*request, ask for*)

Present indicative pido, pides, pide...piden
Present subjunctive pida, pidas, pida, pidamos, pidáis, pidan
Gerund pidiendo
Preterite and imperfect subjunctive pidió, pidieron; pidiera/pidiese

(iii) *Spelling-change verbs*

These are verbs whose spelling has to be adjusted to maintain the correct consonant sound when the ending changes. This therefore only applies to the written language. The changes only apply to the last consonant(s) of the stem and fall into the following main categories [➤2c(v)].

-ar *verbs*
The following changes are necessary before **-e-** throughout the present subjunctive, and in the first person singular only of the preterite:
• a stem ending in **-c-** changes to **-qu-**: **sacar** (take out) becomes **sa*qu*e, sa*qu*es**, etc.; **sa*qu*é**

• a stem ending in **-z-** changes to **-c-**: **empezar** (begin) becomes **empiece, empieces**, etc.; **empecé**
• a stem ending in **-g-** changes to **-gu-**: **pagar** (pay) becomes **pague, pagues**, etc.; **pagué**
• a stem ending in **-gu-** changes to **-gü-**: **averiguar** (verify) becomes **averigüe, averigües**, etc.; **averigüé**

-er *and* **-ir** *verbs*
The following changes are necessary before **-a-** throughout the present subjunctive and before **-o** in the first person singular of the present indicative;
• a stem ending in **-gu-** changes to **-g-**: **seguir** (follow) becomes **siga, sigas**, etc.; **sigo**
• a stem ending in **-g-** changes to **-j-**: **escoger** (choose) becomes **escoja, escojas**, etc., **escojo**

verbs ending in **-uir**
Verbs ending in **-uir** have a **-y-** in the following cases:
• in the singular and third person plural of the present indicative;
• throughout the present and imperfect subjunctives;
• in the third person of the preterite.

concluir (*conclude*)

Present indicative
concluyo concluyes concluye concluimos concluís concluyen

Present subjunctive
concluya concluyas concluya concluyamos concluyáis concluyan

Preterite
concluí concluiste concluyó concluimos concluisteis concluyeron

Imperfect subjunctive
concluyera/concluyese

Also: all other verbs ending in **-ducir**, **huir** (run away), **construir** (build) and all verbs ending in **-struir**, **fluir** (flow) and verbs ending in **-fluir**.

(iv)   *Verbs which add an accent*

A small number of verbs with a stem ending in **-i-** or **-u-** need an accent to stress this vowel in the singular and third person plural of the present.

enviar (*send*)

Present indicative
envío envías envía enviamos enviáis envían

Present subjunctive
envíe envíes envíe enviemos enviéis envíen

actuar (*act*)

Present indicative
actúo actúas actúa actuamos actuáis actúan

Present subjunctive
actúe actúes actúe actuemos actuéis actúen

>   Also: **desviar** (divert), **continuar** (continue)

(v)   *-g- verbs*

>   There is a group of verbs in which the stem of the present
>   indicative contains **-g-** in the first person singular, and there-
>   fore the present subjunctive [►18c(ii)] contains the **-g-** through-
>   out. Some have a perfectly regular present indicative except
>   for the first person.

hacer (*do, make*)
hago haces hace hacemos hacéis hacen

caer (*fall*)
caigo caes, etc.

poner (*put*)
pongo pones, etc.

salir (*go out*)
salgo sales, etc.

traer (*bring*)
traigo traes, etc.

valer (*be worth*)
valgo vales, etc.

>   Others have stem changes.

decir (*say*)
digo dices dice decimos decís dicen

tener (*have*)
tengo tienes tiene tenemos tenéis tienen

venir (*come*)
vengo vienes viene venimos venís vienen

oír (*hear*)
oigo oyes oye oímos oís oyen

> Both sets keep the **-g-** stem unchanged throughout the present subjunctive.

tener (*have*)
tenga tengas tenga tengamos tengáis tengan

decir (*say*)
diga digas diga digamos digáis digan

(vi)   *-zc- verbs*

> Another sizeable group with an irregular first person singular in the present indicative consists of verbs whose infinitive ends in **-ecer**, **-ocer** and **-ucir**. The stem of the first person of the present indicative, and therefore all the present subjunctive, ends in **-zc-**.

parecer (*seem*)

Present indicative
parezco pareces parece parecemos parecéis parecen

Present subjunctive
parezca parezcas parezca parezcamos parezcáis parezcan

> Common **-er** verbs of this type are:

conocer	know	**desaparecer**	disappear
reconocer	recognize	**merecer**	deserve
parecer	seem, appear	**ofrecer**	offer
aparecer	appear		

> and many more ending in **-ecer.** Common **-ir** verbs are:

lucir	shine	**reproducir**	reproduce
conducir	drive	**traducir**	translate
producir	produce		

> and all other verbs ending in **-ducir.**

(vii)   **-oy** *verbs*

> In the following verbs, the first person singular present indicative ends in **-oy**. The present subjunctive is not affected by this.

dar (*give*)
doy das da damos dais dan

estar (*be*)
estoy estás está estamos estáis están (N.B. accents)

Ir (go) is irregular, but the present tense is predictable once established.

voy vas va vamos vais van

(viii) Pretérito grave

A significant group of verbs has what is known as a **pretérito grave**, that is, the first and third person singular preterite [➤18c(vi)] endings are not stressed and bear no accent. These verbs are some of the commonest ones, and the stem of the preterite is usually unpredictable. The other endings are as for **-er/-ir** verbs, although the group includes **andar** and **estar**.

tener (*have*)
tuve tuviste tuvo tuvimos tuvisteis tuvieron

Other verbs with a **pretérito grave** are:

andar	**anduve**	walk	**poder**	**pude**	can
caber	**cupe**	fit	**poner**	**puse**	put
estar	**estuve**	be	**quere**	**quise**	want
haber	**hube**	have	**saber**	**supe**	know
hacer	**hice**	do, make	**venir**	**vine**	come

  (**hizo** in third person singular)

and their compounds [➤18a(iii)].

 When the stem of a *pretérito grave* ends in **-j-**, the third person plural ending is **-eron**.

decir **dije...dijeron** say, tell

traer **traje...trajeron** bring
(*and its compounds*)

conducir **conduje...condujeron** lead, drive
(*and all verbs ending in* **-ducir**).

18c Formation of tenses

In all verbs there are some tenses whose stems and endings can be predicted if you know one of the other parts of the verb. Parts which cannot be predicted in this way have to be learnt, but once these principal parts are known, it is usually possible to predict other parts.

It is helpful to know how to get the stem on to which to put the endings for each tense, and any spelling adjustments that may need to be made. The following sections give a breakdown of the stem and endings for each tense, and any pitfalls to watch out for.

The term *indicative* is used to describe the 'ordinary' tenses, as opposed to the *subjunctive* forms [➤16].

The model regular verbs used in chapters 18 and 19 are: **comprar** (buy), **comer** (eat) and **vivir** (live).

(i) *Present indicative [➤12a]*

- Stem: remove infinitive endings
- Endings

-ar *verbs*

-o -as -a -amos -áis -an

-er *verbs*

-o -es -e -emos -éis -en

-ir *verbs*

-o -es -e -imos -ís -en

➤
- Stem-changing verbs, all types [➤18b(ii)].
- Spelling-changes to final consonant of stem [➤18b(iii)].
- Stem of first person singular only ending in **-g-** (**poner**, etc.) [➤18b(v)]
- Stem of first person singular only ending in **-zc-** (verbs in **-ocer**, **-ecer, -ucir**) [➤18b(vi)].
- Verbs ending in **-uir** (**concluir**, etc.) [➤18b(iii)].
- First person singular of four verbs end in **-oy** (**dar**, **estar**, **ir**, **ser**).
- **Ver**: **veo**, **ves**, etc.
- Other irregular verbs [➤19f].

(ii) *Present subjunctive [➤16]*

- Stem: remove ending from first person singular present indicative.

- Endings: the 'opposite' ones to the indicative, i.e. the vowel is **-e-** for **-ar** and **-a-** for **-er** and **-ir**. Note that the first person singular ends in **-e** (**-ar**) or **-a** (**-er/-ir**).

-ar *verbs*

-e -es -e -emos -éis -en

-er/-ir *verbs*

-a -as -a -amos -áis -an

➤
• Stem-changing verbs, all groups [➤18b(ii)]. Pay particular attention to the further **e → i** and **o → u** change in second and third persons plural, types 2 and 3.
• Spelling-changes to final consonant of stem [➤18b(iii)].
• Stem ends in **-g-** (**poner**, etc.) [➤18b(v)].
• Stem **-zc-** (verbs in **-ocer, -ecer, -ucir**) [➤18b(vi)].
• Verbs ending in **-uir** (**concluir**, etc.) [➤18b(iii)].
• Irregular present subjunctives: **caber → quepa, haber → haya, ir → vaya, saber → sepa, ser → sea** [➤19f].

(iii)   Future [➤14a]

• Stem: add endings to the infinitive. See below for irregular future stems. The endings are the same for all verbs.

• Endings: note the stress accent on all except **-emos**.

-é -ás -á -emos -éis -án

⚠ The following verbs have irregular stems, which, however, all end in **-r-**.

caber	cabré	fit
decir	diré	say
haber	habré	have (*auxiliary*)
hacer	haré	do, make
poder	podré	be able
poner	pondré	put
querer	querré	want, love
saber	sabré	know
tener	tendré	have
valer	valdré	be worth
venir	vendré	come

and also compounds of any of these [➤18e, 19f].

(iv)   Conditional [➤14d]

• Stem: as for future [➤18c(iii)].

• Endings: the same as the **-er/-ir** imperfect [➤18c(v)] but on the future stem.

-ía -ías -ía -íamos -íais -ían

Note   The irregular future stems in 18c(iii) apply to the conditional.

(v)   Imperfect indicative [➤13b]

• Stem: remove infinitive ending.

• Endings:

-ar
-aba -abas -aba -ábamos -abais -aban

-er/-ir
-ía -ías -ía -íamos -íais -íais

 Ser and **ir** have irregular imperfect indicative forms. **Ver** (see) retains the **-e-**: **veía**, etc.

ser (*be*)
era eras era éramos erais eran

ir (*go*)
iba ibas iba íbamos ibais iban

(vi) Preterite [➤13a]

• Stem: remove infinitive ending.

• Endings: note the stressed endings in the first and third persons singular.

-ar
-é -aste -ó -amos -asteis -aron

-er/-ir
-í -iste -ió -imos -isteis -ieron

 • **Pretérito grave** [➤18b(viii)], where the ending of the first and third persons singular are not stressed and the stem can be very irregular.

tener (*have*)
• Stem: **tuv-**
• Endings: -e -iste -o -lmos -isteis -ieron

decir (*say*)
• Stem: **dij-**. Note that there is no **-i-** in third person plural of all verbs of this type with stem ending in **-j-**.
• Endings: -e -iste -o -imos -isteis -eron

There are further irregularities in the following types of verb, which should be checked in the relevant paragraph:
• Stem-changing verbs [➤18b(ii), 19d(ii), (iii)], types 2 and 3.
• Where the **-ieron** ending follows a vowel, **-ll-** or **-ñ-** [➤19e(vi)].
• **Dar**, **ir**, **ser** [➤19f].

(vii) Imperfect subjunctive [➤16]

• Stem: remove ending from third person plural of the preterite.

• Endings: there are two forms of this tense, which are totally interchangeable except in the one instance described in paragraph 14d.

-ar

-ara -aras -ara -áramos -arais -aran

-ase -ases -ase -ásemos -aseis -asen

-er/-ir

-iera -ieras -iera -iéramos -ierais -ieran

-iese -ieses -iese -iésemos -ieseis -iesen

 Any of the stem irregularities mentioned in 18c(vi) on the preterite are carried right through both forms of the imperfect subjunctive.

mentir	mintieron	→	**mintiera** or **mintiese**	lie
dormir	durmieron	→	**durmiera** or **durmiese**	sleep
leer	leyeron	→	**leyera** or **leyese**	read
decir	dijeron	→	**dijera** or **dijese**	say
ir/ser	fueron	→	**fuera** or **fuese**	go, be

(viii) *Compound tenses with **haber** [➤19c]*

The following compound past tenses are formed with the auxiliary verb **haber** (have) + the past participle [➤10d(i)]:

Indicative
• perfect [➤13c];
• pluperfect [➤13d];
• past anterior [➤13e];
• future perfect [➤14b];
• conditional perfect [➤14e];

Subjunctive
• perfect and pluperfect[➤16].

18d   Formation of non-finite parts

(i)   *The imperative [➤15]*

(A) *Informal imperative positive singular (**tú**) [➤23b(i)]*
Stem: remove the final **-s** from second person singular present indicative.

compras	→	compra
comes	→	come
vives	→	vive

Watch out for the following verbs [➤19f].

decir	→	di	salir	→	sal
hacer	→	haz	ser	→	sé
ir	→	ve	tener	→	ten
poner	→	pon	venir	→	ven

(B) *Informal imperative positive plural (**vosotros**)* [➤23b(i)]
Stem: remove **-r** of infinitive and add **-d**. No exceptions, but the **-d-** drops out when the reflexive pronoun **-os** [➤23c(i)] is added. This is one of the only three places where **-er** and **-ir** verbs have different endings.

comprar	→	comprad	buy
comer	→	comed	eat
vivir	→	vivid	live
lavarse	→	lavaos	wash
ponerse	→	poneos	become
divertirse	→	divertíos	enjoy oneself
		N.B. accent on **-í-**	

But:

irse	→	idos	go away

Note In speech, the infinitive is often used: **lavaros, poneros, divertiros, iros.** This is particularly the case with **-ir** verbs.

(C) *Informal negative imperatives and all formal imperatives (**usted** and **ustedes**)* [➤23b(i)]
Stem and endings: use the present subjunctive. Informal ones use the second person and formal ones use the third person endings.

Note Object pronouns are attached to the end of a positive imperative but precede the verb in a negative one [➤23b(iv)].

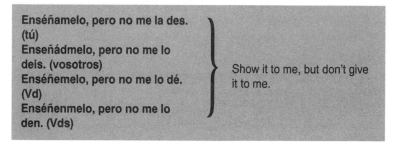

Enséñamelo, pero no me la des.
(tú)
Enseñádmelo, pero no me lo
deis. (vosotros)
Enséñemelo, pero no me lo dé.
(Vd)
Enséñenmelo, pero no me lo
den. (Vds)

Show it to me, but don't give it to me.

• Summary of the imperative

Informal positive singular

compra	come	vive

Informal positive plural

comprad	comed	vivid

Informal negative

no compres	no comas	no vivas
no compréis	no comáis	no viváis

Formal positive

compre Vd	coma Vd	viva Vd
compren Vds	coman Vds	vivan Vds

Formal negative

no compre Vd	no coma Vd	no viva Vd
no compren Vds	no coman Vds	no vivan Vds

 Any irregularity in the present subjunctive will, of course, occur in the imperative where it uses a subjunctive form.

(ii)   Gerund [➤10b, c]

• Stem: remove infinitive ending.

• Endings: **-ando** (**-ar** verbs), **-iendo** (**-er/-ir** verbs).

comprando   comiendo   viviendo

 • If the **-i-** of the ending would be between vowels it becomes **-y-**: **leer**, **leyendo** (read), **oír**, **oyendo** (hear) and others [➤19e(iii), (iv)].
• After **-ll-** and **-ñ-** the **-i-** is dropped: **zambullirse**, **zambulléndose** (dive), **gruñir**, **gruñendo** (grunt).

(iii)   Past participle [➤10d]

• Stem: remove infinitive ending.

• Endings: **-ado** (**-ar** verbs), **-ido** (**-er/-ir** verbs).

comprado   comido   vivido

 Note these irregular past participles:

abrir	**abierto**	open
cubrir	**cubierto**	cover
descubrir	**descubierto**	discover, uncover
decir	**dicho**	say, tell
disolver	**disuelto**	dissolve

escribir	**escrito**	write
freír	**frito**	fry
hacer	**hecho**	make, do
imprimir	**impreso**	print
poner	**puesto**	put
resolver	**resuelto**	solve, resolve
romper	**roto**	break
ver	**visto**	see
volver	**vuelto**	return

and compounds of these.

18e   *Compound verbs*

(i)   *Prefixes:* **des-, re-, mal-**

Prefixes can be added to any base verb so long as it makes sense.

Des- often corresponds to the English 'un-' or 'de-'.

atar	tie	**desatar**	untie
congelar	freeze	**descongelar**	unfreeze, de-ice
cubrir	cover	**descubrir**	discover, uncover
hacer	do	**deshacer**	undo

Re- can be used like the English or French 're-', but take care, as it is not used to the same extent to indicate repetition and is often used to intensify rather than repeat the action.

vender	sell	**revender**	resell
llenar	fill	**rellenar**	fill up, fill out
mojar	wet	**remojar**	soak, drench
quemar	burn	**requemar**	scorch, parch

Mal- gives the meaning of *bad, badly* or *evil.*

gastar	spend	**malgastar**	squander, waste
decir	say	**maldecir**	curse
		(N.B. past participle **maldito**)	
lograr	succeed	**malograrse**	fail, come to grief

(ii)   *-poner, -tener, -venir*

Some common base verbs have a variety of prefixes.

Poner (put) has compounds which often correspond to English verbs ending in '-pose'.

componer	compose
descomponerse	decompose, rot, break down
deponer	depose, lay down (arms, etc.)
imponer	impose
interponer	interpose
posponer	put behind, postpone
proponer	propose, suggest
oponer	oppose
reponer	replace, put back; reply
suponer	suppose
presuponer	presuppose

Tener (have) has compounds which correspond to English verbs ending in '-tain'.

contener	contain
detener	detain, stop
entretener	entertain; hold up, detain
mantener	maintain
retener	retain
sostener	sustain

Venir (come) has a number of compounds.

convenir	agree, suit
intervenir	intervene
provenir	come forth
sobrevenir	happen, occur (unexpectedly)

Satisfacer is a compound of **hacer** and is formed in the same way.

(iii)   -ducir

Sometimes the base verb does not exist: there are several verbs based on **-ducir**, corresponding to English verbs ending in '-duce' or '-duct' but there is no base verb **ducir**.

conducir	conduct, lead, drive
deducir	deduce
inducir	induce, induct
introducir	introduce, insert
producir	produce
reducir	reduce
reproducir	reproduce
seducir	seduce
traducir	translate

19 **Verb tables**

19a   Regular verbs

The three conjugations, or groups, of Spanish verbs which follow a regular pattern have infinitives ending in -**ar**, -**er** and -**ir**. The model verbs we shall use for each group are:

comprar   buy   **comer**   eat   **vivir**   live

Note   Although **vivir** is set out in full, -**ir** verbs only differ from -**er** verbs in three endings: first and second person plural of the present and the **vosotros** imperative.

Unless otherwise stated, the *stem*, i.e. the part of the verb you put the endings on to, is what you are left with when you remove the -**ar**, -**er** or -**ir** of the infinitive.

19b   Regular verbs: simple tenses (one-word tenses)

Present indicative

compro	como	vivo
compras	comes	vives
compra	come	vive
compramos	comemos	vivimos
compráis	coméis	vivís
compran	comen	viven

Present subjunctive

compre	coma	viva
compres	comas	vivas
compre	coma	viva
compremos	comamos	vivamos
compréis	comáis	viváis
compren	coman	vivan

Gerund

comprando	comiendo	viviendo

Present and imperfect progressive
See under *compound tenses* [➤19c(i)].

Imperative (command)

Second person singular informal (**tú**) form, positive only:

compra   come   vive

Second person plural informal (**vosotros**) form, positive only:

comprad   comed   vivid

⚠ All formal (**usted/ustedes**) and all negative commands use the subjunctive.

Second person singular informal (**tú**), negative:

no compres   no comas   no vivas

Second person plural informal (**vosotros**), negative:

no compréis   no comáis   no viváis

Usted and **ustedes** formal forms, positive and negative, use third person endings:

| (no) compre Vd | (no) coma Vd | (no) viva Vd |
| (no) compren Vds | (no) coman Vds | (no) vivan Vds |

Preterite

compré	comí	viví
compraste	comiste	viviste
compró	comió	vivió
compramos	comimos	vivimos
comprasteis	comisteis	vivisteis
compraron	comieron	vivieron

Imperfect indicative

compraba	comía	vivía
comprabas	comías	vivías
compraba	comía	vivía
comprábamos	comíamos	vivíamos
comprabais	comíais	vivíais
compraban	comían	vivían

Imperfect subjunctive

The stem for the imperfect subjunctive is the same as for the third person plural of the preterite: **compr-aron**, **com-ieron**, **viv-ieron**. This is important for many irregular verbs in 18b(ii).

There are two forms of the imperfect subjunctive which are interchangeable except as indicated in 16h(iii).

comprase	comprara	comiese	comiera	viviese	viviera
comprases	compraras	comieses	comieras	vivieses	vivieras
comprase	comprara	comiese	comiera	viviese	viviera
comprásemos	compráramos	comiésemos	comiéramos	viviésemos	viviéramos
compraseis	comprarais	comieseis	comierais	vivieseis	vivierais
comprasen	compraran	comiesen	comieran	viviesen	vivieran

Past participle

comprado	comido	vivido

The past participle is used to form the compound tenses with **haber** [▶19c(ii)].

Future

The stem for the future is the whole infinitive. For exceptions see paragraph 18c(iii). The last syllable is stressed and an accent is needed in all but the first person plural (**-emos**).

compraré	comeré	viviré
comprarás	comerás	vivirás
comprará	comerá	vivirá
compraremos	comeremos	viviremos
compraréis	comeréis	viviréis
comprarán	comerán	vivirán

Conditional

The conditional has the same stem as the future, i.e. the infinitive, and uses the same endings as the -ía form of the imperfect indicative.

compraría	comería	viviría
comprarías	comerías	vivirías
compraría	comería	viviría
compraríamos	comeríamos	viviríamos
compraríais	comeríais	viviríais
comprarían	comerían	vivirían

19c   Regular verbs: compound tenses (two-word tenses)

(i)   Progressive tenses

These are formed with **estar** [▶8d(ii)] (or occasionally **ir** or **venir**) + the gerund [▶10c(ii)]. The present and imperfect are the most commonly used, both in their indicative and subjunctive forms, though other tenses are quite feasible.

Present progressive indicative/subjunctive

estoy/esté comprando	estoy/esté comiendo	estoy/esté viviendo
estás/estés comprando	estás/estés comiendo	estás/estés viviendo
está/esté comprando	está/esté comiendo	está/esté viviendo
estamos/estemos comprando	estamos/estemos comiendo	estamos/estemos viviendo
estáis/estéis comprando	estáis/estéis comiendo	estáis/estéis viviendo
están/estén comprando	están/estén comiendo	están/estén viviendo

Imperfect progressive indicative

estaba comprando	estaba comiendo	estaba viviendo
estabas comprando	estabas comiendo	estabas viviendo
estaba comprando	estaba comiendo	estaba viviendo
estábamos comprando	estábamos comiendo	estábamos viviendo
estabais comprando	estabais comiendo	estabais viviendo
estaban comprando	estaban comiendo	estaban viviendo

Imperfect progressive subjunctive
Formed with **estuviera** or **estuviese**, etc. + the gerund.

Future progressive
Estaré, etc. + gerund.

(ii) Compound tenses with *haber*

Perfect indicative
The perfect is formed with the present of the auxiliary **haber** + the past participle. The past participle does not change.

he comprado	he comido	he vivido
has comprado	has comido	has vivido
ha comprado	ha comido	ha vivido
hemos comprado	hemos comido	hemos vivido
habéis comprado	habéis comido	habéis vivido
han comprado	han comido	han vivido

Perfect subjunctive
Present subjunctive of **haber** + past participle.

haya comprado	haya comido	haya vivido
hayas comprado	hayas comido	hayas vivido
haya comprado	haya comido	haya vivido
hayamos comprado	hayamos comido	hayamos vivido
hayáis comprado	hayáis comido	hayáis vivido
hayan comprado	hayan comido	hayan vivido

Pluperfect indicative
Imperfect indicative of **haber** + past participle.

había comprado	había comido	había vivido
habías comprado	habías comido	habías vivido
había comprado	había comido	había vivido
habíamos comprado	habíamos comido	habíamos vivido
habíais comprado	habíais comido	habíais vivido
habían comprado	habían comido	habían vivido

Pluperfect subjunctive
Imperfect subjunctive (either form) of **haber** + past participle.

hubiera comprado	hubiera comido	hubiera vivido
hubieras comprado	hubieras comido	hubieras vivido
hubiera comprado	hubiera comido	hubiera vivido
hubiéramos comprado	hubiéramos comido	hubiéramos vivido
hubierais comprado	hubierais comido	hubierais vivido
hubieran comprado	hubieran comido	hubieran vivido

(Or with: **hubiese, hubieses, hubiese, hubiésemos, hubieseis, hubiesen.**)

Future perfect
Future of **haber** + past participle.

habré comprado	habré comido	habré vivido
habrás comprado	habrás comido	habrás vivido
habrá comprado	habrá comido	habrá vivido
habremos comprado	habremos comido	habremos vivido
habréis comprado	habréis comido	habréis vivido
habrán comprado	habrán comido	habrán vivido

Conditional perfect
Conditional of **haber** + past participle.

habría comprado	habría comido	habría vivido
habrías comprado	habrías comido	habrías vivido
habría comprado	habría comido	habría vivido
habríamos comprado	habríamos comido	habríamos vivido
habríais comprado	habríais comido	habríais vivido
habrían comprado	habrían comido	habrían vivido

19d Stem-changing verbs

For an explanation of this type of verb, see 18b(ii). Listed below are the full tenses where stem changes occur. If the tense is not listed, the verb is regular in that tense.

(i)   Type 1

Mainly **-ar** or **-er** verbs, a few **-ir**. The stem change is **e** to **ie** or **o** to **ue** (**jugar** only: **u** to **ue**).

| **pensar** | think | **volver** | return | **jugar** | play |

Present indicative

pienso	vuelvo	juego
piensas	vuelves	juegas
piensa	vuelve	juega
pensamos	volvemos	jugamos
pensáis	volvéis	jugáis
piensan	vuelven	juegan

Present subjunctive

piense	vuelva	juegue
pienses	vuelvas	juegues
piense	vuelva	juegue
pensemos	volvamos	juguemos
penséis	volváis	juguéis
piensen	vuelvan	jueguen

Positive informal imperative

| piensa | vuelve | juega |

• Some of the most common type 1 verbs are:

acertar	hit the mark	descender	descend
acordarse	remember	discernir	discern
acostarse	lie down, go to bed	doler	hurt, ache
		empezar	begin, start
adquirir	acquire	encender	light
almorzar	have lunch	entender	understand
atender	attend to, look after	encontrar	find, meet
		enterrar	bury
atravesar	cross	gobernar	govern
calentar	warm, heat	helar	freeze
cerrar	close, shut	inquirir	enquire
comenzar	begin	llover	rain
comprobar	prove, check	morder	bite
concernir	concern	mostrar	show
consolar	console	mover	move
contar	count, tell	negar	deny
defender	defend	nevar	snow
demostrar	demonstrate	oler (N.B. huelo)	smell

probar	prove, try	sonar	sound
recordar	remember	soñar	dream
reforzar	strengthen, reinforce	temblar	tremble, shiver
		tender	tend, stretch
rogar	request, ask	tentar	try, attempt
sembrar	sow	tronar	thunder
sentarse	sit down	volar	fly, blow up

(ii) Type 2

All verbs in this group are **-ir** verbs. There are two stem changes: **e** to **ie** and **i**, **o** to **ue** and **u**.

mentir	lie	dormir	sleep

Present indicative

miento	duermo
mientes	duermes
miente	duerme
mentimos	dormimos
mentís	dormís
mienten	duermen

Present subjunctive

mienta	duerma
mientas	duermas
mienta	duerma
mintamos	durmamos
mintáis	durmáis
mientan	duerman

Positive informal imperative

miente	duerme

Gerund

mintiendo	durmiendo

Preterite

mentí	dormí
mentiste	dormiste
mintió	durmió
mentimos	dormimos
mentisteis	dormisteis
mintieron	durmieron

Imperfect subjunctive

mintiera/mintiese	durmiera/durmiese
mintieras/mintieses	durmieras/durmieses
mintiera/mintiese	durmiera/durmiese
mintiéramos/mintiésemos	durmiéramos/durmiésemos
mintierais/mintieseis	durmierais/durmieseis
mintieran/mintiesen	durmieran/durmiesen

• Some of the commonest type 2 verbs are:

advertir	warn, advise	**hervir**	boil
arrepentirse	repent, be sorry	**morir**	die
convertir	convert	**preferir**	prefer
diferir	defer, differ	**referir**	refer, relate
divertirse	enjoy oneself	**sentir**	feel, be sorry
herir	wound, injure	**sugerir**	suggest

(iii)   Type 3

All verbs in this group are **-ir** verbs. The change is alway **e** to **i**.

pedir   request, ask

Present indicative

pido	pedimos
pides	pedís
pide	piden

Present subjunctive

pida	pidamos
pidas	pidáis
pida	pidan

Positive informal imperative

pide

Gerund

pidiendo

Preterite

pedí	pedimos
pediste	pedisteis
pidió	pidieron

Imperfect subjunctive

pidiera/pidiese	pidiéramos/pidiésemos
pidieras/pidieses	pidierais/pidieseis
pidiera/pidiese	pidieran/pidiesen

• Some of the most common type 3 verbs are:

conseguir	manage to, obtain	**reírse**	laugh
corregir	correct	**reñir**	quarrel, scold
despedir	dismiss, fire, sack	**repetir**	repeat
		seguir	follow
		servir	serve
elegir	elect, choose	**sonreír**	smile
gemir	groan	**teñir**	dye
regir	rule	**vestirse**	dress

19e Spelling-change verbs [➤18b(iii)]

Note Many spelling-change verbs are also stem-changing [➤19d].

(i) -ar verbs

• **c** to **qu**: **sacar** (take out)
Stem ends in -**c**- throughout except:

Present subjunctive

saque saques saque saquemos saquéis saquen

Preterite

saqué sacaste sacó sacamos sacasteis sacaron

Also:

aplicar	apply	**indicar**	indicate, point (out)
atacar	attack		
atracar	assault, mug	**practicar**	practise
buscar	look for, search	**tocar**	touch, play (instrument)
confiscar	confiscate		
educar	educate	**trocar**	change
identificar	identify	**volcar**	upset, turn over

and many more.

• **z** to **c**: **cazar** (hunt)
Stem ends in -**z**- throughout, except:

Present subjunctive

cace caces cace cacemos cacéis cacen

Preterite

cacé cazaste cazó cazamos cazasteis cazaron

Also:

alcanzar	reach, attain	**forzar**	force
almorzar	have lunch	**lanzar**	launch, throw
avergonzarse	be ashamed	**reforzar**	reinforce
comenzar	begin	**rezar**	pray
empezar	begin	**tropezar**	trip
esforzarse	struggle, strive		

and others.

• **g** to **gu**: **pagar** (pay)
Stem ends in **-g-** throughout, except:

Present subjunctive
pague pagues pague paguemos paguéis paguen

Preterite
pagué pagaste pagó pagamos pagasteis pagaron

Also:

cegar	blind	**llegar**	arrive
colgar	hang, hang up	**negar**	deny
descolgar	take down, pick up (phone)	**plegar**	fold
		regar	water, irrigate
desplegar	unfold	**rogar**	ask, request
fregar	wash, scour (dishes)	**sosegar**	calm

• **gu** to **gü**: **averiguar** (verify, check)
Stem ends in **-gu-** throughout, except:

Present subjunctive
averigüe averigües averigüe averigüemos averigüéis averigüen

Preterite
averigüé averiguaste averiguó averiguamos averiguasteis averiguaron

Also:

amortiguar	deaden, muffle	**apaciguar**	pacify, appease

(ii)   *-er* and *-ir* verbs

• **c** to **z**: **torcer** (turn, twist)
Stem ends in **-c-** throughout, except:

Present indicative
tuerzo tuerces tuerce torcemos torcéis tuercen

Present subjunctive
tuerza tuerzas tuerza torzamos torzáis tuerzan

Also:

convencer	convince	**retorcer**	twist, wring
esparcir	scatter, spread	**vencer**	conquer, win

• **gu** to **g**: **distinguir** (distinguish)
Stem ends in **-gu-** throughout, except:

Present indicative
distingo distingues distingue distinguimos distinguís distinguen

Present subjunctive
distinga distingas distinga distingamos distingáis distingan

Also:

conseguir	manage to, obtain	**proseguir**	continue
perseguir	pursue	**seguir**	follow

• **g** to **j**: **escoger** (choose)
Stem ends in **-g-** throughout, except:

Present indicative
escojo escoges escoge escogemos escogéis escogen

Present subjunctive
escoja escojas escoja escojamos escojáis escojan

Also:

coger	catch, seize	**fingir**	feign, pretend
colegir	collect	**proteger**	protect
corregir	correct	**regir**	rule
elegir	elect, choose	**restringir**	restrict

(iii) *Verbs with **-y-** between vowels*

huir (flee, run away): stem ends in **-u-** throughout, except:

Present indicative
huyo huyes huye huimos huís huyen

Present subjunctive
huya huyas huya huyamos huyáis huyan

Informal imperative singular
huye

Gerund
huyendo

Preterite
huí huiste huyó huimos huisteis huyeron

Imperfect subjunctive
huyera/huyese

Also:

construir	build, construct	**excluir**	exclude
destruir	destroy	**incluir**	include
concluir	conclude		

(iv) *Verbs with -y- between vowels, and stressed weak vowel in ending*

leer (read): these verbs behave regularly except:

Gerund
leyendo

Preterite
leí leíste leyó leímos leísteis leyeron

Past participle
leído

Imperfect subjunctive
leyera/leyese

Also:

creer believe

and

caer fall **oír** hear

which have other irregularities [➤19f].

(v) *Verbs with stressed weak vowel (í or ú)*

• **enviar** (send): the -i- is unstressed throughout, except:

Present indicative
envío envías envía enviamos enviáis envían

Present subjunctive
envíe envíes envíe enviemos enviéis envíen

Informal imperative singular
envía

Also:

criar	rear, bring up	**desafiar**	challenge, defy
desviar	divert	**guiar**	guide
fiar	trust	**llar**	bind, tie
confiar	confide	**vaciar**	empty

• **actuar** (act): the **-u-** is unstressed throughout, except:

Present indicative
actúo actúas actúa actuamos actuáis actúan

Present subjunctive
actúe actúes actúe actuemos actuéis actúen

Informal imperative singular
actúa

Also:

continuar	continue	**perpetuar**	perpetuate
insinuar	insinuate		

(vi) *Verbs whose stem ends in -ll- or -ñ-*

The **-i-** of the ending is lost.

• **zambullirse** (dive)

Gerund
zambulléndose

Preterite
me zambullí te zambulliste se zambulló nos zambullimos
os zambullisteis se zambulleron

Also:

engullir	gobble, gulp	**escabullirse**	slip away, bunk

• **gruñir** (grunt)

Gerund
gruñendo

Preterite
gruñí gruñiste gruñó gruñimos gruñisteis gruñeron

Imperfect subjunctive
gruñera/gruñese

Also:

reñir	scold, quarrel	**tañer**	play, pluck
teñir	dye		(instrument)

Note **Reñir** and **teñir** are also type 3 stem-changing verbs.

19f *Irregular verbs*

The following are the most common irregular verbs in Spanish. Only irregularly formed tenses are mentioned. In the future and conditional, only the stem can be irregular – the same endings are always used. Any irregularity in the future will therefore apply to the conditional, so it is not listed separately.

Verbs with a **pretérito grave** [➤18b(viii)] are marked (*pg*). Verbs with a present indicative and subjunctive which follow the stem-change pattern described in 19d are marked (*sc*).

---

abrir *open*

Past participle
abierto

---

andar *walk*

Preterite (*pg*)
anduve anduviste anduvo anduvimos anduvisteis anduvieron

Imperfect subjunctive
anduviera/anduviese

---

caber *fit, be contained*

Present indicative
quepo cabes cabe cabemos cabéis caben

Present subjunctive
quepa quepas quepa quepamos quepáis quepan

Future
cabré

Preterite (*pg*)
cupe cupiste cupo cupimos cupisteis cupieron

Imperfect subjunctive
cupiera/cupiese

caer *fall*

Present indicative
caigo caes cae caemos cais caen

Present subjunctive
caiga caigas caiga caigamos caigáis caigan

Gerund
cayendo

Past participle
caído

Preterite
caí caíste cayó caímos caísteis cayeron

Imperfect subjunctive
cayese/cayera

---

conducir *drive, lead*

Present indicative
conduzco conduces conduce conducimos conducís conducen

Present subjunctive
conduzca conduzcas conduzca conduzcamos conduzcáis conduzcan

Preterite (pg)
conduje condujiste condujo condujimos condujisteis condujeron

Imperfect subjunctive
condujera/condujese

Also all verbs ending in **-ducir**.

---

cubrir *cover*

Past participle
cubierto

Also **descubrir** (discover).

---

dar *give*

Present indicative
doy das da damos dais dan

Present subjunctive
dé des dé demos deis den

Preterite
di diste dio dimos disteis dieron

Imperfect subjunctive
diera/diese

---

decir *say, tell*

Present indicative
digo dices dice decimos decís dicen

Present subjunctive
diga digas diga digamos digáis digan

Informal imperative singular
di

Gerund
diciendo

Future
diré

Past participle
dicho

Preterite (*pg*)
dije dijiste dijo dijimos dijisteis dijeron

Imperfect subjunctive
dijese/dijera

---

escribir *write*

Past participle
escrito

---

estar *be*

Present indicative
estoy estás está estamos estáis están

Present subjunctive
esté estés esté estemos estéis estén

Preterite (*pg*)
estuve estuviste estuvo estuvimos estuvisteis estuvieron

Imperfect subjunctive
estuviera/estuviese

freír *fry*

Past participle
frito

Otherwise a type 3 stem-changing verb [▶18b(ii), 19d]

haber *have* (as auxiliary)

Present indicative
he has ha hemos habéis han

Present subjunctive
haya hayas haya hayamos hayáis hayan

Future
habré

Preterite *(pg)*
hube hubiste hubo hubimos hubisteis hubieron

Imperfect subjunctive
hubiera/hubiese

 When it means 'there is/are', the third person singular present indicative is **hay**. In other tenses the normal third person singular is used.

hacer *do, make*

Present indicative
hago haces hace hacemos hacéis hacen

Present subjunctive
haga hagas haga hagamos hagáis hagan

Informal imperative singular
haz

Future
haré

Past participle
hecho

Preterite *(pg)*
hice hiciste hizo hicimos hicisteis hicieron

Imperfect subjunctive
hiciera/hiciese

imprimir *print*

Past participle
impreso

---

ir *go*

Present indicative
voy vas va vamos vais van

Present subjunctive
vaya vayas vaya vayamos vayáis vayan

Informal imperative singular
ve

Gerund
yendo

Preterite
fui fuiste fue fuimos fuisteis fueron

Imperfect subjunctive
fuera/fuese

---

oír *hear*

Present indicative
oigo oyes oye oímos oís oyen

Present subjunctive
oiga oigas oiga oigamos oigáis oigan

Gerund
oyendo

Preterite
oí oíste oyó oímos oísteis oyeron

Imperfect subjunctive
oyera/oyese

---

poder *be able, can*

Present indicative (sc)
puedo puedes puede podemos podéis pueden

Present subjunctive (sc)
pueda puedas pueda podamos podáis puedan

Gerund
pudiendo

Future
podré

Preterite (pg)
pude pudiste pudo pudimos pudisteis pudieron

Imperfect subjunctive
pudiera/pudiese

---

poner put

Present indicative
pongo pones pone ponemos ponéis ponen

Present subjunctive
ponga pongas ponga pongamos pongáis pongan

Informal imperative singular
pon

Future
pondré

Past participle
puesto

Preterite (pg)
puse pusiste puso pusimos pusisteis pusieron

Imperfect subjunctive
pusiera/pusiese

Also all compounds [➤18e].

---

querer want, love

Present indicative (sc)
quiero quieres quiere queremos queréis quieren

Present subjunctive (sc)
quiera quieras quiera queramos queráis quieran

Future
querré

Preterite (pg)
quise quisiste quiso quisimos quisisteis quisieron

Imperfect subjunctive
quisiera/quisiese

---

resolver *resolve*

Past participle
resuelto

Otherwise stem-changing, type 1.

Also **absolver** (absolve), **disolver** (dissolve).

---

romper *break*

Past participle
roto

---

saber *know*

Present indicative
sé sabes sabe sabemos sabéis saben

Present subjunctive
sepa sepas sepa sepamos sepáis sepan

Future
sabré

Preterite (*pg*)
supe supiste supo supimos supisteis supieron

Imperfect subjunctive
supiera/supiese

---

salir *go/come out*

Present indicative
salgo sales sale salimos salís salen

Present subjunctive
salga salgas salga salgamos salgáis salgan

Informal imperative singular
sal

Future
saldré

ser *be*

Present indicative
soy eres es somos sois son

Present subjunctive
sea seas sea seamos seáis sean

Informal imperative singular
sé

Imperfect indicative
era eras era éramos erais eran

Preterite
fui fuiste fue fuimos fuisteis fueron

Imperfect subjunctive
fuera/fuese

---

tener *have*

Present indicative (sc)
tengo tienes tiene tenemos tenéis tienen

Present subjunctive
tenga tengas tenga tengamos tengáis tengan

Informal imperative singular
ten

Future
tendré

Preterite (pg)
tuve tuviste tuvo tuvimos tuvisteis tuvieron

Imperfect subjunctive
tuviera/tuviese

---

traer *bring*

Present indicative
traigo traes trae traemos traéis traen

Present subjunctive
traiga traigas traiga traigamos traigáis traigan

Gerund
trayendo

Preterite (*pg*)
traje trajiste trajo trajimos trajisteis trajeron

Imperfect subjunctive
trajera/trajese

---

venir *come*

Present indicative (*sc*)
vengo vienes viene venimos venís vienen

Present subjunctive
venga vengas venga vengamos vengáis vengan

Informal imperative singular
ven

Gerund
viniendo

Future
vendré

Preterite (*pg*)
vine viniste vino vinimos vinisteis vinieron

Imperfect subjunctive
viniera/viniese

Also all compounds [➤18e].

---

ver *see*

Present indicative
veo ves ve vemos veis ven

Present subjunctive
vea veas vea veamos veáis vean

Imperfect indicative
veía

Past participle
visto

---

volver *return*

Past participle
vuelto
Otherwise a stem-changing, type 1 [➤18b(ii), 19d].
Also **devolver** (return, give back), **envolver** (wrap), **revolver** (stir up).

D

PEOPLE, THINGS AND IDEAS: NOUNS AND NOUN PHRASES

20 Labelling the world: nouns

20a   What does a noun do?

Nouns answer the questions **¿Quién es?** (Who is it?) and **¿Qué es?** (What is it?). They are the labels we attach to everything in the world around us or in our own minds: people, animals, things, events, processes, ideas.

Mi *hija* menor estudia *física* en la *universidad*.	My youngest *daughter* is studying *physics* at *university*.

20b   Adding details: the noun phrase

The noun phrase often consists of more than just a noun – it is extended so as to provide more information. The additional words and phrases which supply this information are:

• determiners [➤21];
• adjectives and adjectival phrases [➤22];
• relative clauses [➤5b, 23k];
• prepositional phrases [➤25b, c].

To avoid repetition, noun phrases are often represented by pronouns [➤23].

20c   Individual names and general labels: 'proper' and 'common' nouns

A *proper noun* (or *proper name*) is the name of a particular individual person, animal, place or thing. All other nouns are *common nouns*. Proper nouns in Spanish always begin with a capital letter, except:

• names of days, months and seasons;
• titles.

Mi hija *Julia* estudia física en la universidad de *Salamanca*.	My daughter *Julia* is studying physics at *Salamanca* University.

Empezó sus estudios en octubre. El *sábado* que viene vamos a visitarla. Su tutora se llama la *señora Calderón*. Es una universidad famosa: la han visitado recientemente los *reyes* de España.	She began her studies in *October*. We're going to visit her next *Saturday*. Her tutor's name is *Mrs.Calderón*. It's a famous university: it has been visited recently by the *King and Queen* of *Spain*.

20d Classes of Spanish noun: genders

The word *gender* means *kind* or *type*. There are only two genders in Spanish – *masculine* and *feminine*. As there is no neuter gender, this means that all Spanish nouns are categorized into masculine or feminine, whether they are living creatures or not. The gender of a noun may often be established by meaning or by ending. We recommend learning nouns with the definite article **el** (masculine) or **la** (feminine) [▶21c(i)] to help the gender stick in your mind, and nouns in the following examples are shown with their article.

20e Gender by meaning

(i) General

(A) In the case of human beings and common domestic animals and a few others, male beings are of course masculine, and female ones feminine.

Masculine		*Feminine*	
el hombre	man	**la mujer**	woman
el hijo	son	**la hija**	daughter
el tío	uncle	**la tía**	aunt
el panadero	baker (male)	**la panadera**	baker (female)
el toro	bull	**la vaca**	cow
el perro	dog	**la perra**	bitch
el león	lion	**la leona**	lioness

However, the word for most animals has no relevance to the sex of the animal.

| **el ratón** | mouse | **la rata** | rat |
| **el oso** | bear | **la girafa** | giraffe |

(B) Many fruit trees are masculine, and their fruit feminine.

el cerezo	cherry tree	**la cereza**	cherry
el manzano	apple tree	**la manzana**	apple

(ii) Other masculine nouns include:

(A) Rivers, oceans, seas, lakes, mountains, regardless of ending: **el Guadiana**, **el Paraná**, **el Atlántico**, **el Caribe**, **el Titicaca**, **el Teide**.

(B) Numbers, months and days: **un 75 por ciento** (75 per cent), **el martes** (Tuesday), **el próximo octubre** (next October).

(C) Infinitives of verbs [➤10a(iii)]: *el fumar* **es malo para la salud** (smoking is bad for the health).

(iii) Other feminine nouns include:

(A) Letters of the alphabet: **una g**, **una m**.

(B) Islands, as **la(s) isla(s)** (feminine) is understood: **las Canarias** (Canaries).

(C) Medical terms ending in **-osis** or **-itis**: **la diagnosis** (diagnosis), **la apendicitis** (appendicitis).

20f Gender by ending

(i) *-o, -a masculine, feminine*

In many of the above examples you will have noticed that the nouns ending in **-o** are masculine, and those ending in **-a** are feminine. This is indeed the case with most Spanish nouns ending in **-o** and **-a**.

el bolígrafo	ballpoint	**la carta**	letter
el brazo	arm	**la pierna**	leg

 With some nouns, the **-o**/**-a** ending not only changes the gender but also changes the meaning.

el libro	book	**la libra**	pound (sterling and weight)
el puerto	port	**la puerta**	door
el naranjo	orange tree [➤20e(i)]	**la naranja**	orange

(ii) Exceptions

There are some exceptions to the general rule, however.

(A) Nouns ending in **-o** which are feminine include:

la foto	photo	**la radio**	radio
la mano	hand	(masculine in Spanish America)	
la moto	motorbike		

(B) Nouns ending in **-a** which are masculine include many ending in **-ma**:

el anagrama	anagram	**el pijama**	pajama
el fantasma	ghost	**el programa**	program
el clima	climate	**el sistema**	system
el crucigrama	crossword	**el síntoma**	symptom
el drama	drama	**el telegrama**	telegram
el esquema	plan	**el tema**	theme, topic
el panorama	panorama		

(C) All nouns ending in **-ista**, which is invariable.

el/la ciclista	cyclist	**el/la derechista**	right-winger
el/la comunista	communist		(politician)
el/la futbolista	footballer		

(Many of these may also be used as adjectives [➤22a].)

(D) Those ending in **-cida** are masculine.

el insecticida	insecticide	**el suicida**	suicide

(E) Those ending in a stressed vowel are masculine.

el champú	shampoo	**el sofá**	sofa, settee

(F) And also:

el mapa	map	**el tranvía**	tram, slow train,
el planeta	planet		stopping train
		el yoga	yoga

(iii) Other endings

Other endings can also indicate gender.

(A) Masculine

• Nouns ending in **-aje**:

| **el aprendizaje** | apprenticeship | **el paisaje** | countryside |
| **el garaje** | garage | | |

- Nouns ending **-or**:

| **el color** | color | **el valor** | value |

but *la* **labor** (work, labor), *la* **flor** (flower), which are feminine.

- Compound nouns:

| **el parachoques** | bumper, fender | **el rascacielos** | skyscraper |

(B) Feminine

- Nouns ending in **-ión**:

| **la estación** | station, season | **la revolución** | revolution |
| **la misión** | mission | | |

but *el* **camión** (lorry, truck), *el* **avión** (plane), *el* **gorrión** (sparrow).

- Nouns ending in **-dad, -tad**, **tud**:

| **la bondad** | goodness, kindness | **la voluntad** | will |
| | | **la virtud** | virtue |

- Nouns ending in **-umbre**:

| **la cumbre** | summit, peak | **la incertidumbre** | uncertainty |

- Nouns ending in **-ie**:

| **la superficie** | surface |

- Nouns ending in **-is**:

| **la crisis** | crisis |

but **el análisis** (analysis), **el énfasis** (emphasis), **el écstasis** (ecstasy) and a few others, which are masculine.

- Countries and regions are feminine if they end in unstressed **-a**. Otherwise they are usually masculine.

| (la) España | (la) Argentina | (la) Andalucía | |
| (el) Canadá | (el) Méjico | (el) Perú | (el) Aragón |

The article is in fact not often used with countries and regions [➤21c(iv)].

20g   One or more? Singular and plural

(i)   -s, -es

The rule for making most nouns plural in Spanish is very simple:

nouns ending in an unstressed vowel or stressed -é add **-s**, and those ending in a consonant or other stressed vowel add **-es**.

Tengo dos *hijas* en *universidades* diferentes. Mis dos *hijos* son *dueños* de varios *cafés*.	I have two *daughters* in different *universities*. My two *sons* are *owners* of several *cafés*.

(ii)   Exceptions

There are a few exceptions, however:

(A) Nouns ending in unstressed **-es** or **-is**, and compound nouns [▶3a(i)] ending in **-s** do not add anything.

el lunes	los lunes	Monday(s)
la crisis	las crisis	crisis/crises
el rascacielos	los rascacielos	skyscraper(s)

(B) The following nouns ending in a stressed vowel add **-s**.

la mamá	las mamás	mom/moms (mum/mums)
el menú	los menús	menu(s)
el papá	los papás	pop/pops (daddy/daddies)
el tisú	los tisús	tissue(s)

(C) Some other nouns ending in a stressed vowel which correctly form their plural by adding **-es** are often heard in speech with **-s** only.

el rubí	los rubíes/rubís	ruby/rubies

(D) Foreign words usually add -s regardless of the rules

el barman	los barmans	barman/men
el coñac	los coñacs	cognac(s)

unless the word would be rendered unpronounceable, in which case **-es** or nothing is added.

el sandwich	los sandwiches/sandwich	sandwich(es)

(iii)   Spelling changes

Some plurals are affected by spelling changes [▶2c(v)]:

(A) Nouns ending in **-z** change this to **-c-** before **-es.**

una vez	dos veces	once/twice

(B) Nouns with a stress accent on the final syllable lose the accent when **-es** is added.

el inglés	los ingleses	Englishman/the English
la estación	las estaciones	station(s); season(s)

(C) Nouns ending in **-en** which are stressed on the next to last syllable need an accent when **-es** is added.

el examen	los exámenes	exam(s)

(D) Note also two nouns which change their stress in the plural:

el carácter	los caracteres	character(s)
el régimen	los regímenes	regime(s), diet(s)

20h   *Adjectives used as nouns*

(i)   Lo + adjective

An adjective can be made into a sort of noun representing the 'quality' of the adjective, by the use of the pronoun **lo** [➤23e(ii)]. It is really an abbreviated form of **lo que es** (that which is).

Lo interesante es que mis hijas son unas académicas y mis hijos empresarios. *Lo importante* es que cada uno encuentre un trabajo que le guste. *Lo inquietante* sería que no lo encontrara/encontrasen.	*The interesting part* is that my daughters are academics and my sons entrepreneurs. *The important thing* is that they find a job that they enjoy. *The worrying thing* would be if they couldn't find one.

(ii)   Los + adjective

In a similar way, the adjective can be used with a plural article referring to a category of person or thing.

los grandes y *los buenos*	*the great* and *the good*

(iii)   Colors

When a color is used as a noun, it is masculine.

El rojo **es mi color preferido, pero me gusta también** *el azul.*	*Red* is my favorite color, but I also like *blue.*

Note An adjective can be used agreeing with an absent but understood noun.

De estas faldas prefiero *las rojas* **a** *las azules.*	Of these skirts, I prefer *the red (ones)* to *the blue (ones).*

20i   Nouns formed from other parts of speech

(i)   Infinitives as nouns

The infinitive of a verb may be used as a noun [➤10a(iii)] and is often the equivalent of the English form ending in '-ing'.

Comer **muchos caramelos es malo para los dientes.**	*Eating* a lot of candies is bad for the teeth.

➤ It is frequently used in this way after verbs such as **gustar** (like) and **apetecer** (fancy) [➤8h(v)].

A mis hijos no les gusta *estudiar*, **pero a ambas hijas les** *apeteció ir* **a la universidad.**	My sons don't like *studying*, but both daughters wanted *to go* (liked the idea of *going*) to university.

(ii)   Abstract nouns

These can be formed from verbs, adjectives and other nouns, but there are few firm rules which can be given as regards their formation.

(A) There are many nouns ending in **-ción** or **-sión**, usually denoting an action or process derived from a verb.

crear	to create	**la creación**	creation
perder	to lose	**la perdición**	perdition
promover	to promote	**la promoción**	promotion
dimitir	to resign	**la dimisión**	resignation

(B) Another 'verb-to-noun' ending is **-miento**.

llamar	to call, appeal	**el llamamiento**	appeal
nombrar	to name	**el nombramiento**	nomination

(C) Qualities derived from an adjective or a noun often end in **-dad**, **-tad**, and sometimes **-tud**. The former often correspond to English words ending in '-ty'.

bueno	good, kind	**la bondad**	kindness
nacional	national	**la nacionalidad**	nationality
libre	free	**la libertad**	freedom, liberty
precoz	precocious	**la precocidad**	precociousness

(D) Nouns are also formed with the ending **-umbre**.

mucho(s)	much, many	**la muchedumbre**	crowd, rabble
cierto	certain	**la certidumbre**	certainty

(E) Some are formed with the ending **-ez**.

niño	child	**la niñez**	childhood
pálido	pale	**la palidez**	paleness

(F) Other endings are **-eza**, **-ura**.

bello	beautiful	**la belleza**	beauty
hermoso	beautiful	**la hermosura**	beauty

(iii)   Noises and actions

(A) Animal and other noises mostly convert from verb to noun by the ending **-ido**.

ladrar	to bark	**el ladrido**	bark
maullar	to meow	**el maullido**	meow
rugir	to roar	**el rugido**	roar
sonar	to sound	**el sonido**	sound

(B) Some actions derived from verbs end in **-ada** or **-ida**.

ir	go	**la ida**	(action of) going
llegar	to arrive	**la llegada**	arrival
parar	to stop	**la parada**	(e.g. bus) stop
salir	to go out, leave	**la salida**	exit, departure

21 Specifying nouns: determiners

21a What are determiners?

You will not find the word *determiner* in older grammars, but it is a very useful term, which takes in some of the most common words in any language. Unlike ordinary adjectives, determiners do not describe nouns but are used to place them in a context, to say whether they are assumed to be known or not, to whom they belong, how many there are, and so on. Determiners come first in a noun phrase, taking the same gender and number as the noun. Most determiners have corresponding pronouns, which replace the whole noun phrase [▶20b]. (Numerals are also determiners, but it is convenient to discuss them separately in chapter 28.)

21b The interrogative determiner: Which?

This is the question word listed in paragraph 6d(iii).

¿En *qué* universidad estudia su otra hija?	*Which* university is your other daughter studying at?

21c Already known: the definite article 'the'

When the definite article is used, we know precisely what the noun refers to, because it has already been mentioned, because it is closely defined or because it is obvious. When the phrase also contains an adjective, it answers the question ¿**Qué...?** (Which...?) [▶6d(iii)].

(i) el los la las

The definite article has four non-interchangeable forms in Spanish: masculine singular (**el**) and plural (**los**), feminine singular (**la**) and plural (**las**).

Los hijos trabajan en Valladolid, *el* menor en *el* centro y *el* mayor en *las* afueras; *las* hijas están en *la* universidad de Salamanca.	*The* sons work in Valladolid, *the* younger in *the* center and *the* elder in *the* suburbs; *the* daughters are at *the* University of Salamanca.

(ii)   *el* + *feminine nouns beginning with stressed* ***a-*** *or* ***ha-***

The masculine article **el** is used for the sake of the sound before feminine nouns beginning with stressed **a-** or **ha-** in the singular.

Salamanca es hermosa, ¡aunque *el agua* del río Tormes no es muy clara!	Salamanca is beautiful, though *the water* of the Tormes River isn't very clear!

(iii)   *al* and *del*

When preceded by the prepositions **a** (to, at) or **de** (of, from), the masculine singular **el** forms the only two such contractions in Spanish, **al** (to/at the) and **del** (of/from the).

(iv)   *Non-use of definite article*

The definite article is not used:

(A) With numbers of Popes, monarchs, etc.

El rey actual de España es *Juan Carlos primero.*	The present king of Spain is *Juan Carlos the First.*

(B) With the names of most countries, except when they are qualified by an adjective [➤21c(iii)].

Hoy en día *España* es muy distinta de *la España del siglo* XIX.	Nowadays *Spain* is very different from *19th-century Spain.*

Some Latin American countries may have the article (**el Perú**), but this is becoming increasingly optional, and even **Estados Unidos** without **los** is becoming common, though strictly any country with a 'made-up' name should have the article.

(C) A noun in apposition [▶3c] is not normally preceded by the definite article.

Lima, *capital* de Perú	Lima, *the capital* of Peru

(v) Use of definite article

The definite article is used:

(A) When referring to nouns in a general sense, i.e. the whole of a particular group or an idea in general.

Los españoles son famosos por la acogida que dan a *los extranjeros.* Para ellos *la amistad* es importante.	*(The) Spaniards* are famous for the welcome they give to *foreigners.* For them *friendship* is important.

(B) With titles when referring to the person in question, but not when addressing them directly.

– Buenos días, *señora* Ramírez. Veo que *el rey* Juan Carlos y *el presidente* Felipe González van a visitar esta ciudad este año.	"Good morning, *Mrs.* Ramírez. I see that *King* Juan Carlos and *President* Felipe González are going to visit this town this year."

(C) With a proper name [▶20c] when it is qualified by an adjective.

Mi hija Isabel es un buen ejemplo para *la joven Carmencita.*	My daughter Isabel is a good example for *young Carmencita.*

(D) With parts of the body and clothing, the possessor often being the indirect object of the verb [▶8f(iii), 21g(vi)].

Abre *la boca.* Te voy a examinar *la dentadura.*	Open *your mouth.* I'm going to inspect *your teeth.*

(E) When expressing percentages, although the indefinite article **un** [▶21e] may also be used.

El/un 90 por ciento de los que van al dentista tienen que ser atendidos.	*Ninety per cent* of those who go to the dentist have to have treatment.

(F) With weights and measures, to express *per* kilo, litre, etc.

Los tomates están a 100 pesetas *el* kilo.	Tomatoes are 100 pesetas *per (a) kilo.*

(G) To express *on* a day or date [▶30c].

Tengo que ir al dentista *el nueve* de enero. No trabaja *los sábados*.	I have to go to the dentist *on the ninth* of January. He doesn't work *on Saturdays.*

(H) With **de** to express possession [▶23j(ii)].

Mi casa y *la de mi hermano*.	My house and *my brother's.*

21d Pointing and showing: demonstrative determiners 'this', 'that'

Demonstratives are like a strong definite article. They refer to something very specific, usually indicating whether it is near to or far from the speaker in time and place. Spanish has three demonstratives:

• **este** *this* (near the speaker);
• **ese** *that* (near the person addressed);
• **aquel** *that* (over there, away from both the speaker and the person addressed).

Masculine

este libro	this book	**estos libros**	these books
ese libro	that book	**esos libros**	those books (near you)
aquel libro	that book	**aquellos libros**	those books (over there)

Feminine

esta revista	this magazine	**estas revistas**	these magazines
esa revista	that magazine	**esas revistas**	those magazines (near you)
aquella revista	that magazine	**aquellas revistas**	those magazines (over there)

Quisiera una botella de *este* **vino, dos botellas de** *esa* **cerveza, y ¿cuánto cuesta** *aquella* **sidra?**	I'd like a bottle of *this* wine, two bottles of *that* boor (by you), and how much is *that* cider (over there)?
Póngame un kilo de *estos* **tomates, medio kilo de** *esas* **cebollas y de** *aquellas* **uvas.**	Give me a kilo of *these* tomatoes, half a kilo of *those* onions (by you) and of *those* grapes (over there).

In expressions of time, **aquel** is used to denote the remote past.

¿Los años treinta? ¡En *aquella* **época yo ni siquiera había nacido!**	The Thirties? I wasn't even born in *those* days!

For the pronoun form of the demonstrative and its use to mean *the former* and *the latter,* see paragraph 23h.

21e *Unknown individuals: the indefinite article 'a (an)'*

When the indefinite article is used, we know what type of person or thing the noun refers to but not which individual. When the phrase also contains an adjective, it answers the question **¿Qué tipo/clase de...?** (What kind of?) [➤6d(iv)].

(i) *Un una*

The indefinite article in Spanish is **un** for masculine nouns and **una** for feminine nouns.

Acabo de comprar *un* **periódico y** *una* **revista.**	I've just bought *a* newspaper and *a* magazine.

 The same rule applies as with the definite article [➤21c(ii)]: before a feminine noun beginning with stressed **a-** or **ha-** use the masculine form.

Para cortar el árbol necesitamos *un hacha*.	To cut down the tree we need *an axe*.

(ii)   *Non-use of the indefinite article*

The use of the indefinite article in Spanish is often much the same as in English, but there are a number of occasions where it is not used.

(A) After **ser** (be), **hacerse** (become), **sentirse** (feel), etc. with a noun complement denoting a profession, occupation, rank or nationality, unless the noun is qualified by an adjective or other phrase which makes it stand out from its class.

Mi hija quiere *hacerse abogada*. Su novio *es portugués. Es político*. **Mi hija quiere *hacerse una abogada famosa*. Su novio *es un portugués muy simpático*. *Es un político de tendencias liberales*.**	My daughter wants to *become a lawyer*. Her fiancé *is (a) Portuguese*. He *is a politician*. My daughter wants to *become a famous lawyer*. Her fiancé *is a very nice Portuguese man*. He *is a politician of liberal leanings*.

(B) It is often not used before the direct object of **tener**, **llevar**, **comprar**, **sacar**, **hay** and similar verbs.

¿Hay *problema*? – No, ahora que tengo *coche* ¡hay *solución*!	Is there a problem? –No, now that I have *a car*, there's *a solution*!

(C) After **ser**.

Es *cuestión* de saber dónde comprarlo.	*It's a question* of knowing where to buy one.

(D) Usually before the object of a negative verb.

No tengo *coche* y *no veo posibilidad* de tenerlo.	I *don't have a car* and I *don't see any possibility* of having one.

(E) Before a noun in apposition [▶3c].

Granada, *ciudad histórica* del sur de España	Granada, *a historic city* in the south of Spain

(F) Usually after **sin** (without), and often after **como** (as), and **con** (with).

Estaba con abrigo pero *sin sombrero.*	He *was wearing a coat* but *no hat.*

(G) After ¡qué...! in exclamations (what a...!), before **tal** (such a), **medio** (half a), **otro** (another) and usually **cierto** (a certain).

¡Qué rollo! Tenían *medio kilo* de aquel queso, pero yo quería *otro tipo.* Hay *cierto tipo* que me gusta. Nunca he tenido *tal problema* para conseguirlo.	*What a drag!* They had *half a kilo* of that cheese, but I wanted *another kind.* There's *a certain kind* I like. I've never had *such a problem* getting it.

21f How much? How many?: the indefinite quantifiers 'some', 'all', etc.

Like the indefinite article, quantifiers do not identify specific individuals. Some refer to the whole or none of some thing or group, others to some part or some members of it.

(i) 'Some' and 'any'

• The Spanish for *some* is **alguno**, which has a singular as well as a plural form and the usual adjectival agreements [➤22a(i)], and can be used as a determiner or a pronoun. Note that the masculine singular shortens to **algún** before a noun.

Tendremos que consultar *algún* diccionario de español.	We shall have to consult *some* Spanish dictionary.

• Another equivalent of *some* is the plural form of the indefinite article, **unos/unas**, which can be used in the same way with a plural noun, but is possibly not as emphatic and tends to lean towards *a few* [➤21f(ix)].

Hay *unos* diccionarios en la biblioteca.	There are *some* (a few) dictionaries in the library.

• When there is no great emphasis on the idea of *some* or *any,* and the phrase is merely expressing an indefinite quantity of an article or product, no quantifier is used.

¿Tienen diccionarios de español en la biblioteca? ¿Qué desea Vd? –Quiero *pan, mantequilla, queso y vino*, por favor. ¿Hay *vino* de Rioja?	*Do they have (any) Spanish dictionaries* in the library? What would you like? –I'd like *some* bread, *some* butter, *some* cheese and *some* wine, please. Is there *any* Rioja wine?

• *Any* in its widest sense is **cualquier**.

Lo encontrarás en *cualquier* diccionario.	You'll find it in *any* dictionary.

(ii) Ninguno

Not any, no, none are expressed by **ninguno**. It is the negative of **alguno** in paragraph (i) above, and has the same agreement pattern, although the plural is not often used. Like all negative words, if it follows the verb, the verb is preceded by **no**.

Ningún diccionario es tan bueno como éste. ¿Diccionarios en la biblioteca? *No* tengo *ninguna* idea. *No* hay *ningún* diccionario que sirva.	*No dictionary* is as good as this one. Dictionaries in the library? I have *no* idea. There is *no* dictionary that is any use.

• If there is no great emphasis on the negative quantity of an article or product, then, again, no quantifier is used.

Lo siento, pero *no* tenemos *mantequilla.*	I'm sorry, we have *no* butter/we *don't* have *any* butter.

• On the other hand, the negative can be emphasized by using **alguno** after the noun.

| **No encontré diccionario *alguno*.** | I found *no* dictionary (at all). |

(iii) Todo

All is expressed by **todo**.

| ***Todos* nuestros vinos son de Jumilla.** | *All* our wines are from Jumilla. |
| **He estado *todo el día* en la biblioteca.** | I've been in the library *all* day. |

• **Todo** + a singular noun means *each* or *every*.

| ***Todo* diccionario es propiedad de la biblioteca.** | *Every dictionary* is the property of the library. |

(iv) Cada

Each, every are more usually expressed by **cada** which does not change and takes a singular noun.

| ***Cada* día voy a la bibioteca.** | *Each/every* day I go to the library. |
| **He buscado *cada* palabra que no entendía.** | I've looked up *each/every* word I didn't understand. |

(v) Both

Both is **ambos/ambas** or **los dos/las dos**.

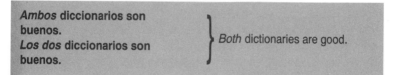

| ***Ambos* diccionarios son buenos.** | } *Both* dictionaries are good. |
| ***Los dos* diccionarios son buenos.** | |

 Do not confuse this use of 'both' with **tanto...como...** (both...and...).

(vi) Mucho

Mucho, which has the usual adjectival forms, means *much, many, a lot*.

| Hay *mucho* trabajo que hacer y *muchas* palabras españolas que no conozco. | There is *a lot of* work to do and *many/lots of* Spanish words I don't know. |

(vii)   Desmasiado

Demasiado means *too much, too many*.

| Hay *demasiados* estudiantes en la biblioteca. | There are *too many* students in the library. |

• **Demasiado** is also an invariable adverb meaning *too* [➤26b, 27b(ii)].

| Este trabajo es *demasiado* difícil. | This work is *too* difficult. |

(viii)   Varios

Varios/varias means *several*, and is of course always plural.

| Utilizo *varios* diccionarios. | I use *several* dictionaries. |

(ix)   Poco

Poco means *not much, little, a little, a few* and agrees in the usual way. It is the opposite of **mucho**, and used in the same way.

| Hay *pocos* buenos diccionarios en esta biblioteca. | There are *few* good dictionaries in this library. |
| Tengo *poco* trabajo que hacer. | I've got *little* (*not much*) work to do. |

(Spanish often prefers to use **poco** where in English we would say *not much*.)

 Be careful to distinguish between **poco** which has a negative connotation and means 'not much', and **un poco de** [➤23i(i)] and **unos pocos**, which mean '*a* little' and '*a* few' respectively, and have a more positive emphasis.

Encontré *pocos* diccionarios en la biblioteca.	I found *few* dictionaries in the library.
Encontré *unos pocos* diccionarios en la biblioteca.	I found *a few* dictionaries in the library.
Se encuentra *poca ayuda* en la biblioteca.	You find *little* help in the library.
Hoy me dieron *un poco de* ayuda.	Today they gave me *a little/a bit of* help. [▶23i(i)]

(x)   Tanto

Tanto/tantos mean *so much, so many*.

Hay *tantas palabras* que aprender.	There are so many words to learn.

(xi)   Más and menos

More and *less*: *more* is **más** and *less* is **menos**. They are both invariable, that is, they never change, and generally present few problems in their use. *More and more/less and less* are **cada vez más/cada vez menos**.

Me hacen falta *más* días libres y *menos* trabajo, porque estudio *cada vez más*.	I need *more* days off and *less* work, because I study *more and more*.

For further uses of **más/menos** with comparatives, see paragraph 22d(i).

The more...the more, the more...the less... and *the less...the less...* are rendered by **cuanto más (menos)... más (menos)...**

Cuantos más diccionarios busco, *menos* encuentro.	*The more dictionaries* I look for, *the fewer* I find.

21g   Belonging together: possessive determiners

Possessives are used to show that the noun belongs to somebody or something. They take their form from the possessor, and their gender and number from the thing possessed. The words *belong* and *possess* are used loosely here: possessives are also used for all kinds of other relationships between people and things, as in *your family, my home town, its members*.

(i) *Spanish possessive determiners (short form)*

	Thing possessed	
Possessor	*Singular*	*Plural*
my	**mi**	**mis**
your (belonging to **tú**)	**tu**	**tus**
his	**su**	**sus**
her	**su**	**sus**
its	**su**	**sus**
your (belonging to **Vd**)	**su**	**sus**
our	**nuestro/nuestra**	**nuestros/nuestras**
your (belonging to **vosotros**)	**vuestro/vuestra**	**vuestros/vuestras**
their	**su**	**sus**
your (belonging to **Vds**)	**su**	**sus**

Toda *mi familia* vive en esta región, *mis tíos*, *mis primos*, y *mis hermanos*.	All *my family* live in this area, *my uncles and aunts, my cousins, my brothers and sisters.*
Mi marido es de Andalucía. *Su hermana* vive aquí también, pero *sus padres* y *sus otros hermanos* viven en el sur.	*My husband* is from Andalusia. *His sister* lives here as well, but *his parents* and *his other brothers and sisters* live in the south.

(ii) *Your*

Be careful to distinguish between the different words for *your*, as they are *not* interchangeable.

¿Has escrito recientemente a *tus* padres?	Have you (**tú**) written lately to *your* parents?
¿Habéis escrito recientemente a *vuestros* padres?	Have you (**vosotros**) written lately to *your* parents?
¿Ha escrito Vd recientemente a *sus* hijos?	Have you (**Vd**) written lately to *your* children?
¿Han escrito Vds recientemente a *sus* hijos?	Have you (**Vds**) written lately to *your* children?

(iii)   *Su sus*

Remember that **su** and **sus** can mean *his, her, its, your* (**Vd**), *their* or *your* (**Vds**), and that the *plural* form **sus** is used with the *things possessed*.

Su hijo can mean *his/her/your* (**Vd/Vds**)/*their son,* i.e. only *one* son, whoever he belongs to!

Sus hijos can mean *his/her/your* (**Vd/Vds**)/*their sons:* two or more sons, whoever they belong to!

(iv)   *Avoiding ambiguity*

The obvious question is: doesn't this lead to ambiguity at the least, and total confusion at worst, as to what belongs to whom? The answer is: not often, as the sense is usually obvious from the context.

El señor Alonso escribe a *su* **hijo.**	Mr. Alonso is writing to *his* son.
La señora Alonso escribe a *su* **hijo.**	Mrs. Alonso is writing to *her* son.
Los Alonso escriben a *su* **hijo.**	The Alonsos are writing to *their* son.
Señor Alonso, ¿cuándo va Vd a escribir a *su* **hijo?**	Mr. Alonso, when are you going to write to *your* son?
¿Cuándo van Vds a escribir a *su* **hijo?**	When are you (i.e. both) going to write to *your* son?

(v)   *de* + *disjunctive pronoun*

If the correct 'possessor' is not clear, **de** + the disjunctive pronoun [▶23f(v)] is added to the person or thing possessed. Usually in this case, the possessive **su/sus** is replaced by the definite article [▶21c], as it is now superfluous.

¿Cuándo van Vds a escribir *a su hijo*? **¿Cuándo van Vds a escribir** *al hijo de ella*?	When are you going to write to *her* son?

In the first example above, you would only know the **su** meant *her* if you were already talking about the woman in question. Otherwise it would mean *your son.* In the second version, it is clear that it is *her son.*

El señor Alonso va a escribir a *su hijo.* El señor Alonso va a escribir *al hijo de Vds.*	Mr Alonso is going to write *to your son.*

Again, in the first example, only the context would indicate that the **su** means *your* rather than *his*. This ambiguity is removed in the second version.

(vi)   Body and clothes

The possessive is not normally used with actions performed to parts of the body or clothing, where the indirect object pronoun [▶8f(iii), 23b(iii)] identifies the possessor.

Le estreché *la mano.*	I shook *his/her* hand.

(vii)   The 'long' form of the possessive: **mío**, etc.

The 'long' form of the possessive without the definite article can also be used as a determiner.

mío	mía	míos	mías	mine
tuyo	tuya	tuyos	tuyas	yours (**tú**)
suyo	suya	suyos	suyas	yours (**Vd**)
suyo	suya	suyos	suyas	his, hers
nuestro	nuestra	nuestros	nuestras	ours
vuestro	vuestra	vuestros	vuestras	yours (**vosotros**)
suyo	suya	suyos	suyas	yours (**Vds**)
suyo	suya	suyos	suyas	theirs

(A) After **ser** to indicate possession.

Estas maletas son *mías* y creo que las otras son *suyas,* ¿no? Esta no es *nuestra.* Tiene que ser *suya.*	These suitcases are *mine* and I believe the others are *yours* (**Vds**), aren't they? This one isn't *ours.* It must be *yours.*

(B) Meaning *of mine*, *of theirs*, etc. in phrases such as:

Son unos amigos nuestros.	They are *friends of ours.*

Note   If the correct possessor cannot be assumed, **de** + the disjunctive
pronoun is used as in (v) above.

Estas maletas son mías, y creo que las otras son *de Vds*, ¿no?	These suitcases are mine, and I believe the others are *yours*, aren't they?

22 Describing nouns: adjectives

22a   What do adjectives do?

Adjectives describe noun phrases. They can be used either as part of a phrase containing a noun [➤22b] or in the predicate of the sentence [➤22c].

(i)   Agreement of adjectives

Spanish adjectives agree in gender and number with the noun(s) they describe.

(A) The many adjectives ending in **-o** have four forms: masculine singular and plural, feminine singular and plural.

un **periódico nuevo**	a new paper	**periódicos nuevos**	new papers
una **revista nueva**	a new magazine	**revistas nuevas**	new magazines

(B) Most of those ending in a consonant or **-e** do not have a separate feminine form, simply a plural. Add **-s** to those ending in **-e**.

un techo verde	a green roof	**techos verdes**	green roofs
una pared verde	a green wall	**paredes verdes**	green walls

Add **-es** to those ending in a consonant.

un techo azul	a blue roof	**techos azules**	blue roofs
una pared azul	a blue wall	**paredes azules**	blue walls

 Adjectives of nationality and region do have a feminine form, singular and plural and are spelled without an initial capital letter [➤2c(vi)].

un pueblo francés	a French village	**pueblos franceses**	French villages
una ciudad francesa	a French city	**ciudades francesas**	French cities

Sevilla y Córdoba son *ciudades* *andaluzas.*	Seville and Córdoba are *Andalusian cities.*

 Adjectives ending in **-or**, and also in **-án**, **-ón** and **-ín** also have a feminine form.

Elvira es una mujer mandon*a*, charlatan*a*, pero puede ser encantador*a*.	Elvira is a bossy, talkative woman, but she can be charming.

(ii)   Agreement: exceptions

(A) The series of *comparative* adjectives, which simply add **-es** in the plural.

mejor	better	**anterior**	previous, earlier
peor	worst	**posterior**	later
mayor	greater, elder	**exterior**	outer
menor	smaller, younger	**interior**	inner
superior	upper	**ulterior**	last, ultimate
inferior	lower		

Esta es una de *las mejores* películas españolas – mucho mejor que *las anteriores*.	This is one of the *best Spanish movies* – much better than *the earlier* ones.

(B) Adjectives ending in **-a**, e.g. **belga** (Belgian), and all those ending in **-ista** [▶20f(ii)] do *not* end in **-o** in the masculine.

El Partido Social*ista*	The Socialist Party

 Colors which are taken from the name of a flower or fruit remain invariable.

El piso tiene alfombras *violeta* y paredes *rosa*.	The apartment has *violet* carpets and *pink* walls.

The *great* and the *good:* adjectives used as nouns [▶20h].
A *skillful* writer writes *skillfully:* adverbs formed from adjectives [▶26b(i)].

22b   Accompanying the noun: attributive adjectives

Attributive adjectives form part of the same phrase as a noun, though sometimes the noun is *understood*, that is, left out because it is obvious [▶22b(v)].

(i)   *Normal position of adjectives*

The adjective normally follows the noun in Spanish.

> **Preferimos el *vino tinto*, sobre todo si es un *vino riojano*.**   We prefer *red wine*, especially if it is a *Rioja* wine.

However, some common adjectives often precede the noun, especially **bueno** (good) and **malo** (bad).

The following adjectives 'shorten' when they come before a *masculine singular* noun. **Grande** shortens to **gran** before *any* singular noun.

bueno	**buen**	good
malo	**mal**	bad
primero	**primer**	first [➤28b(i)]
tercero	**tercer**	third
alguno	**algún**	some, any [➤21f(i)]
ninguno	**ningún**	no, not any, none
grande	**gran**	big, great
Santo	**San**	saint [➤20c]

(**San** is strictly a title, and a noun, but it is convenient to include it here.)

> **La Rioja es una *gran* región, una de las *grandes* regiones vinícolas de España.**   The Rioja is a *great* region, one of the *great* wine-growing regions of Spain.
> **El *primer* vino es un *buen* ejemplo de *algún* intento de aumentar la producción.**   The *first* wine is a *good* example of *some* attempt to increase production.

(ii)   *Adjectives whose meaning is affected by position*

Some adjectives change their meaning according to whether they are placed before or after the noun.

	Before noun	After noun
antiguo	former, ancient	ancient, old
bueno	kind, good	good
cierto	(a) certain	certain, sure
diferente	sundry, various	different (not the same)
grande	great (important), big	big, large,

medio	half	average, mean
pobre	poor, wretched	poor (no money)
varios	several	various

Por *diferentes razones* hay *cierto sabor* que distingue un *vino bueno.*
Por desgracia, un *hombre pobre* como yo tiene que beber *vino malo.*

For *various reasons* there is a *certain taste* which distinguishes a *good wine.*
Unfortunately a *poor man* like me has to drink *bad wine.*

(iii) Adjectives as part of a phrase

When an adjective is part of a phrase and has no distinguishing force, it usually precedes the noun.

Desde el avión veíamos los *altos rascacielos* de Nueva York.

From the plane we could see the *tall skyscrapers* of New York.

(Tall skyscrapers are a well-known feature of New York: **los rascacielos altos** would have referred to the *tall* skyscrapers as opposed to others which are not tall.)

(iv) Algo, alguien, nada, nadie + adjective

After **algo** (something), **alguien** (someone), **nada** (nothing) and **nadie** (no one) [▶23i(i)] the adjective takes a masculine singular agreement.

¡Una botella de «Gran Reserva» sería *algo especial* para *alguien importante*!

A bottle of "Gran Reserva" would be *something special* for *someone important!*

(v) 'Understood' noun

When the noun is understood, the adjective continues to agree with it as if it were there.

Yo prefiero los vinos tintos a *los blancos.*

I prefer red wines to *white ones.*

22c   *At a distance: predicative adjectives*

(i)   *What is a predicative adjective?*

Predicative means *in the predicate* [➤4c]. These adjectives are usually the complement of the verb, that is, they are linked to the subject by a verb such as those in paragraph 8c, but they can also form separate phrases. Care must be taken to use the correct verb to be – **ser** or **estar** [➤8d(iii)].

El vino que compramos en la tienda de la esquina no era *español*, era *asqueroso*; estaba muy *azucarado*. Como *estábamos* cansados queríamos tomar una copa y acostarnos. ¡Nos acostamos *enfadados y frustrados*!	The wine we bought in the shop on the corner was not *Spanish*, it was *vile*; it was very *sweet*. As we were tired, we wanted to have a glass and go to bed. We went to bed *angry and frustrated*!

A predicative adjective can also be used in formal style instead of an adverb [➤26b(i)].

(ii)   *Tener* + *physical state*

A number of physical states which are described by adjectives in English are the noun object of **tener** in Spanish. The main ones are:

tener calor	be hot, warm (referring to people)
tener frío	be cold (referring to people)
tener razón	be right
tener suerte	be lucky
tener sueño	be sleepy
tener hambre	be hungry
tener sed	be thirsty

(iii)   *Weather*

The same thing happens in weather expressions using **hace** and **hay**.

hace calor	the weather is hot, warm
hace frío	the weather is cold
hace sol	it is sunny
hace viento	it is windy
hay niebla	it is foggy

Because **calor,** etc. are nouns and not adjectives, *very* is translated by **mucho**, which of course agrees with the noun.

Estábamos enfadados porque teníamos mucha sed. ¡Hacía mucho calor aquel día!	We were angry because we *were very thirsty. It was very hot* that day!

22d More and most: comparative and superlative

Most (though not all) adjectives can be used to make comparisons: for this we use the *comparative* form. If we are comparing more than two people or things, then we use the *superlative*.

(i) Comparative

The comparative in Spanish is formed by putting **más** (more) before the adjective and **que** (than) after it, where necessary.

El vino de Rioja es *más famoso* en el extranjero *que* el de Jumilla. No sé cuál es *más fuerte*, pero el Jumilla es *más barato*.	Rioja wine is *more famous* abroad *than* Jumilla. I don't know which is *stronger*, but Jumilla is *cheaper*.

• Four adjectives have their own comparatives without the use of **más**, although **más grande** (larger) and **más pequeño** (smaller) are also used.

bueno	good	**mejor**	better
malo	bad	**peor**	worse
grande	large	**mayor**	larger, *also* older, elder (of people)
pequeño	small	**menor**	smaller, *also* younger (of people)

• In addition it is worth noting that the comparative of **mucho** is **más**, and of **poco** is **menos**.

Siempre he bebido *mucho* vino, pero ¡parece que últimamente bebo *más* cerveza! Siempre he bebido *poco* vino, pero ahora bebo aun *menos*.	I've always drunk *a lot of* wine, but it seems that recently I'm drinking *more* beer! I've always drunk *little* wine, but now it seems I drink even *less*.

• When comparison is made with a number or quantity, **de** is used for *than*.

Debe de haber *más de mil* tipos de vino en España. *Más de la mitad* deben de ser tintos.	There must be *more than a thousand* types of wine in Spain. *More than half* must be red.

• When the comparison of quantity is made with a clause, **de** is also used + **el/la/los/las que** [23k(ii)] if the comparison is with a noun or pronoun, and + **lo que** [23k(vi)] if not.

El proceso es *más complicado de lo que* esperaba. Producen *más vino del que* pensaba. (i.e. *del vino que* pensaba).	The process is *more complicated than* I was expecting. They produce *more wine than* I thought.

(ii)   Superlative

The superlative is formed by using the definite article + the comparative, which may come before or after the noun, or may stand without the noun if it is understood. Note, however, that the article is *not* repeated (as it is in French) when the adjective follows the noun.

El Rioja es *el* vino *más popular* de todos, pero *el más barato* es el Jumilla.	Rioja is *the most popular* wine of all, but *the cheapest* is Jumilla.

• No article is used after a possessive determiner + noun [➤21g(i)].

Mi vicio *más agradable* es el vino.	My *most pleasant* vice is wine.

• After a superlative, use **de** for *in*.

Esa bodega tiene *los mejores vinos de* la ciudad.	That wineshop/liquor store has *the best wines* in town.

(iii)   Negative comparatives and superlatives

The negative comparative and superlative are formed in exactly the same way with **menos** (less, least).

| Encuentro el Jumilla *menos agradable que* el Rioja, pero el vino *menos apetecible de todos* es el que hace mi hijo en casa. | I find Jumilla *less pleasant than* Rioja, but the *least appetizing of all* is the one my son makes at home. |

(iv)   Tan...como...

Another way of comparing people or things is by the so-called comparison of equality, using **tan...como...** (as...as...), or **no tan...como...** (not so...as...) in the negative.

| El vino de mi hijo es *tan bueno como* la mayoría de los vinos caseros, pero *no es tan fuerte como* el mío. | My son's wine is *as good as* most home-made wines, but it is *not as strong as* mine. |

To compare **mucho(s)** in this way, you use **tanto/tantos** (as much/as many) + **como** (as).

| Yo no hago *tanto* vino *como* mi hijo. | I don't make *as much* wine *as* my son. |

(v)   -ísimo

To say something is *very*, *extremely*, etc. + adjective, you can add **-ísimo** to the adjective after removing the **-o**. The **-ísimo** ending agrees with the noun in the usual way. Remember that some adjectives need spelling adjustments before adding **-ísimo** (**rico**, **riquísimo**) [➤2c(v)].

| ¡Esta es una bodega *carísima!* ¡¡Pero los vinos que vende son *riquísimos!!* | This is an *extremely* expensive wine shop. But the wines they sell are *very, very good*!! |

(vi)   Cuanto más...más...The more...the more...

The more...the more, *the less...the less*, *the more...the less* are the relevant combination of **cuanto más/menos... más/menos...**.

Cuanto más vino **hago en casa,** **menos vino compro en la tienda.**	*The more wine* I make at home, *the less wine* I buy in the shop.

➤   All the comparative forms dealt with in this chapter except **tanto...como** are applicable to adverbs [➤26b(iii)].

22e   *Adjectives formed from other parts of speech*

(i)   *Adjectives from nouns*

In Spanish, as in other Latin languages, you cannot use a noun as an adjective in the way that you can in English and German (purchasing power, wine industry): you can either use a noun phrase (**el poder de compra**, **la industria del vino**) or you have in some way to convert the noun to an adjective by giving it an adjectival ending. There is no shortage of this sort of adjective, especially in modern journalistic Spanish. The main problem is the lack of a system to determine the ending to put on the noun, and also that the ending may well be on a different noun from the obvious one. It is often simpler for the learner of Spanish – and purists might argue better style – to use a noun phrase [➤20b]. The following examples illustrate both possibilities.

la industria vinícola	**la industria del vino**	the wine industry
la experiencia laboral	**la experiencia del trabajo**	work experience
la formación ocupacional	**la formación para el trabajo**	job training
el poder adquisitivo	**el poder de compra**	purchasing power
el empleo juvenil	**el empleo de los jóvenes**	youth employment
la vida familiar	**la vida de familia**	family life

(ii)   *Adjectives from verbs*

Adjectives may be formed from verbs. For the Spanish equivalent of English verbal adjectives ending in '-ing' (running water, etc.), and '-ed' or '-en' (a broken window, etc.) see paragraph 10c(v).

22f   *Making adjectives negative*

In English, we often make the opposite, usually the negative, of an adjective by using the prefixes 'un-' or 'dis-', as in *unhappy* or *discontent*. In Spanish, the prefixes **in-** and **des-** exist, as in **infeliz** and **descontento**, but they are not used to the same extent, and if you are not sure of the existence of this form, check in a dictionary. Often other devices are used, of which the most common are:

- **Poco** with the adjective.

Encuentro este vino *poco interesante*.	I find this wine *uninteresting*.

- For 'un-' + a past participle, **sin** + infinitive.

Emplea un método *sin probar*.	He's using an *untried* method.

23 Representing nouns: pronouns

23a What pronouns do

The word *pronoun* means 'in place of a noun'. Pronouns are used instead of nouns as a way of avoiding clumsy repetitions. The types of pronoun discussed in paragraphs 23g to 23j below have corresponding determiners [▶21].

Pronouns take:

• their *gender* (masculine/feminine) and *number* (singular/plural) from the noun they refer to (although Spanish has a number of neuter pronouns which are explained in paragraph 23e below);
• their *form* from their function in the sentence they are in.

23b Personal pronouns

These are the most neutral pronouns – they simply replace nouns without adding further information. They may refer to the person(s) speaking, the person(s) spoken to, or the person(s) spoken about. The pronouns differ in form depending on whether they are the subject, direct object, indirect object or are used independently of a verb, e.g. after a preposition.

(i) Subject pronouns

Singular

First person	**yo**	I
Second person	**tú**	you (*informal*)
	usted (Vd)	you (*formal*)
Third person	**él**	he
	ella	she
	ello	it, this, the fact

Plural

First person	**nosotros/nosotras**	we
Second person	**vosotros/vosotras**	you (*informal*)
	ustedes (Vds)	you (*formal*)
Third person	**ellos**	they (*masculine or mixed*)
	ellas	they (*feminine*)

Because the subject – the doer – of the action [➤4b] is contained in the verb ending in Spanish, the subject pronouns are only used for emphasis, contrast or to avoid confusion, and when they stand alone. **Usted/ustedes** are perhaps used more frequently, mainly because of the possible ambiguity over the shared third person verb endings, but also sometimes to emphasize deference to the person(s) addressed.

¿Qué *vas* a hacer esta tarde? –Esta tarde *yo* iré de compras mientras *tú* te quedas con los niños. *Ella* va de compras. mientras *él* se queda en casa con los niños. ¿Quién quiere ir de compras? ¡*Nosotros*!	What are you going to do this afternoon? –This afternoon *I* will go shopping while *you* stay with the children. *She* is going shopping while *he* stays at home with the children. Who wants to go shopping? *We do*!

 Although **usted** and **ustedes** have been listed under the second person, it is very important to remember that they not only take the third person of the verb, but that in *all other functions* they take *third person pronouns* and *possessives* [➤21g, 23b, 23j]. The reason for this is that **usted** is a much shortened version of the old **vuestra merced**, meaning 'Your Grace'. The same form in English would use the third person: 'If Your Grace *wishes* to learn Spanish, here is *his* Handbook'. **Usted** is often abbreviated in writing to **Vd** or **Ud**, and **ustedes** to **Vds** or **Uds**.

Nosotros, **vosotros** and **ellos** have feminine forms **nosotras**, **vosotras** and **ellas**. When referring to a mixture of sexes the masculine form is used.

• **Formal and informal address**
In Spain in the last couple of decades, the use of the familiar forms **tú** and **vosotros** has become very widespread, particularly among the younger generation. A reasonable guideline is that people on a first name basis would use the informal form. If you were addressing a person as **señor/señora/señorita** or the more old-fashioned **don/doña** you would certainly use **usted/ustedes**. This is somewhat dangerous ground for foreigners and unless you are addressing someone very young, who obviously warrants **tú**, your safest bet is to use **usted** until you are invited to do otherwise! **Vosotros/as** is not used in Spanish America, where the plural form for *you* is **ustedes** regardless of the degree of formality, and the use of the informal singular **tú** is more restricted.

| ¿*Vienen Vds* con nosotros? | *Are you coming* with us? |

¿**Vienen con nosotros?** *could* mean 'Are *they* coming with us?'.

• **Ello**, the neuter subject pronoun, is used to refer to an idea and means *it*, *this*, *that* or *the fact, t*hough its use tends to be literary and **esto** is preferred in speech.

| **Se trata de aceptar una nueva realidad territorial.** *Ello* **equivale a recompensar las depuraciones étnicas.** | It's a question of accepting a new territorial reality. *That* is the equivalent of rewarding ethnic cleansing. |

(ii) Direct object pronouns [➤8e]

Singular

me	me
te	you (*informal*)
le/lo	you (*formal masculine*)
la	you (*formal feminine*)
le/lo	him
lo	it (*for masculine things*)
la	her/it (*for feminine things*)

Plural

nos	us
os	you (*informal*)
les/los	you (*formal masculine*)
las	you (*formal feminine*)
les/los	them (*masculine people*)
los	them (*masculine things*)
las	them (*feminine people and things*)

Both **le** and **lo** are used for the masculine direct object 'him', **lo** tending to be favored in Spanish America and southern Spain. The corresponding plurals are **les** and **los** (them). The same pronouns – with the same choice – are used as the direct object form of **usted** and **ustedes**. The feminine direct objects of **Vd** and **Vds** are, of course, **la** and **las**.

• If the meaning of a third person object pronoun is ambiguous, it is clarified by adding **a** + the disjunctive pronoun [➤23f].

| ¿**Los niños?** ¡*Los* (*les*) **dejo contigo esta tarde!** ¿*Me* **oyes?** –¡**Claro que** *te* **oigo!... Pero ¿dónde está Carmencita? No** *la* **encuentro! Bueno, niños,** *os* **veo sobre las seis.** | The children? I'm leaving *them* with you this afternoon! Do you hear *me*? –Of course I can hear *you*!... But where's Carmencita? I can't find *her*! Right, children, I'll see *you* around six. |

¡Buenas tardes! señora Pérez. Quisiéramos invitar*la* a cenar con nosotros mañana, y si su marido puede acompañar*la*, claro que también *le* invitamos *a él*.	Good afternoon Mrs.Pérez. We would like to invite *you* to dine with us tomorrow, and if your husband is able to accompany *you*, of course we are inviting *him* as well.

(iii)   Indirect object prouns [➤8f]

Singular

me	to me
te	to you (*informal*)
le	to him, to her; to you (*formal*)

Plural

nos	to us
os	to you (*informal*)
les	to them; to you (*formal*)

• Although the indirect object means *to* or *for* someone, in English this is not always clear, and care should be taken to use the correct object pronoun in Spanish.

Los vecinos llamaron. No *me* dijiste que *les* habías llamado. Querían decir*nos* que quieren que *les* prestes tu cargador de baterías.	The neighbors phoned. You didn't tell *me* that you had phoned *them*. They wanted tell (say to) *us* that they want you to lend *(to) them* your battery charger.

• When there is both an indirect and a direct object pronoun, the indirect always precedes the direct [➤8f(iv)].

 When the indirect and direct object pronouns are both third person and would therefore both begin with 'l', the indirect changes to **se**, which is invariable.

No *te lo* dije porque sé que odias a la señora Pérez y no sabía si querías prestár*selo*. —¡Claro que *se lo* presto a él, pero ¡nunca *se lo* presto *a ella*!	I didn't tell *you (it)*, because I know you detest Mrs.Pérez and I didn't know if you would lend *them it*. —Of course I'll lend *it to him*, but I'll never lend *it to her*!

(iv)   Position of object pronouns

All object pronouns precede the verb except the imperative positive (DO it! [➤18d(i)], the infinitive [➤10a], and the gerund

[►10b], where they are attached to the end of the verb. The pronouns may, however, precede an auxiliary or modal verb [►9b] used with the infinitive or gerund. The object pronoun added to the end of the verb becomes part of one word. Therefore, to maintain the correct stress, the gerund and most imperatives need an accent [►2c(i)] on the stressed vowel when any pronoun is added, and the infinitive when two pronouns are added.

¡No! ¡No voy a prestár*selo*! (¡No *se lo* voy a prestar!)	No, I'm not going to lend them (him/her) it!
¿*Me* estás diciendo (estás diciéndo*me*) que vas a montar un follón?	Are you telling *me* that you're going to cause a quarrel?
¡Présta*selo*, por favor!	Lend *it to them*, please!

(v) 'Redundant' object pronouns

Noun objects, both direct and indirect, are often 'doubled' in Spanish by the addition of the object pronoun, especially – but not necessarily – when the object precedes the verb.

¡Ya *les* he prestado este aparato *a los Pérez* dos veces!	I've already lent this gadget *to the Pérezs* twice!
¡Y *mi sierra me la* rompieron!	And they broke *my saw* for me!

See also *Avoidance of passive* [►17e(ii)].

23c Reflexive pronouns

(i) Use of reflexive pronouns

Reflexive pronouns are personal pronouns which refer back to the subject of the sentence, as when you do something to yourself. In the first person (**me**, me; **nos**, us), and the second person (**te**, you; **os**, you *informal*), Spanish uses the normal personal object pronouns as reflexives. But there is a special third person reflexive which is both singular and plural: **se**, which means *himself/herself*, *themselves*, and also *yourself* and *yourselves* for **usted** and **ustedes**, which – remember! – use *third person pronouns*.

If you use the ordinary third person object pronouns **lo/le**, **la**, **los/les**, **las** (him, her, them), then the action is being done to someone else, not to the subject.

Se compró una botella de vino.	*He/she bought himself/herself* a bottle of wine.
Le compró una botella de vino.	*He/she bought him/her* a bottle of wine.

Note Actions performed to parts of one's own body or clothing are usually expressed by a reflexive verb rather than a possessive [►21c(v), 21g(vi)].

Me corté *el* dedo.	*I* cut *my* finger.
Se lavó *la* cara.	*She* washed *her* face.

There is also a third person reflexive disjunctive pronoun **sí**, which means *him/herself, oneself, themselves, yourself/selves* (**Vd/Vds**) [►23f(iv)]. With **con** this becomes **consigo**.

(ii) *'Each other'*

Plural reflexive pronouns can also be used *reciprocally*, that is, when people do something not to themselves but to each other.

Hace ya unas semanas que la señora Pérez y yo *no nos hablamos*.	For some weeks now Mrs.Pérez and I *haven't spoken to each other*.
Por eso mi mujer y yo *nos miramos* extrañados cuando me llamó por teléfono.	So my wife and I *looked at one another* in surprise when she phoned me.

 Do not confuse reflexives with the words we use to emphasize that it was *the subject* that did something, not anyone else. To obtain this emphasis, simply use **mismo** (self), agreeing in gender and number, after the subject pronoun [►23b(i)].

Lo hizo *ella misma*.	She did it *herself*.

23d   The indefinite pronoun 'one'

(i)   Se

To express the idea of the English indefinite pronoun *one*, *you*, *they*, *people* in a general sense (c.f. French *on*), Spanish normally uses the third person reflexive pronoun **se** with the third person singular of the verb.

Se ve que es un problema. *No se sabe* lo que *se debería* hacer. ¿Si *se va* a la policía? Pero no *se quiere* hacer tales cosas.	*One can see* that it's a problem. *One doesn't know* what *one should do*. If *one goes* to the police? But *one doesn't want* to do such things. (*You can see...* , etc. would be an equally good English equivalent.)

(ii)   Uno

The subject pronoun **uno** (one) is normally used only with a reflexive verb, when **se** is already in use as the true reflexive pronoun. It can be used in other circumstances, but sounds rather stilted.

Uno no se atreve a hacer nada.	*One doesn't dare* do anything.

For how to say *I was told* and further comment on the use of **se**, see paragraph 17e.

23e   Neuter pronouns

(i)

There are a number of Spanish pronouns which are used when a masculine or feminine gender cannot be given to what they represent – usually an idea or concept, but sometimes an object which has not yet been identified. These include:

• demonstrative pronouns **esto, eso, aquello** [▶23h];
• the subject and disjunctive pronoun **ello** [▶23b, 23f(iii)];
• the pronoun **lo**.

(ii)   Lo

Lo is used:

(A) As a neuter object or complement [►8c] in cases where English would omit it or perhaps use *so*.

El problema es difícil. Quizás **Vds** *no lo crean*, **pero les** **aseguro que** *lo es*.	The problem is a difficult one. Perhaps you *may not think so*, but I assure you that *it is (so)*.

(B) + **que** to introduce a noun clause, meaning *that which*, *what*, or a relative clause, meaning *which* referring to an idea [►5b], when **lo cual** is also possible.

Lo que **encontramos difícil es el dinero.**	*What* we find difficult is the money.
No tenemos el dinero, *lo que/* *cual* **plantea un gran problema.**	We don't have the money, *which* poses a big problem.

(C) Before an adjective describing an abstract idea or one aspect of something, where it converts it to a kind of noun, and is a shortened version of **lo que es** [►20h(i)].

Lo difícil **es el dinero.**	*The difficult thing* is the money.

(D) In the phrase **lo de**, meaning *the matter of*.

Lo del dinero **nos preocupa** **bastante.**	*The business of the money* worries us a lot.

(E) + an adjective + **que** + verb, meaning *how* in noun clauses and exclamations [►24a]. Regardless of the neuter pronoun, the adjective agrees with the noun it describes.

Vd no sabe *lo difícil que* **es** **encontrar este dinero.**	You don't know *how difficult it is* to find this money.
¡*Lo difíciles que son* **estos** **problemas!**	*How difficult* these problems are!

(iii)   *It*

The English 'impersonal' subject pronoun *it* has no real equivalent in Spanish, as the subject is contained in the verb ending.

There are, nevertheless, plenty of impersonal verbs, such as the weather expressions **hace calor** (it's hot) and expressions such as **hay que** (it's necessary to), **es imposible** (it is impossible to). These are dealt with fully in paragraph 8h.

23f Prepositions and personal pronouns: 'disjunctive' pronouns

Disjunctive means here *not related directly to the verb*. These pronouns are sometimes also called *prepositional* pronouns since their main use is after prepositions.

Singular		Plural	
mí	me	**nosotros**	us
ti	you (informal)	**vosotros**	you (informal)
usted (Vd)	you (formal)	**ustedes (Vds)**	you (formal)
él	him	**ellos**	them (masculine or
ella	her		mixed)
ello	it (referring to idea)	**ellas**	them (feminine)

(i) Note that except for **mí** and **ti**, the form is the same as the subject pronouns in 23b(i).

Siempre vamos teniendo problemas *con ellos*. ¿Qué harían *sin nosotros*? No tengo nada *contra él*, pero la señora Pérez *delante de ti* dijo ciertas cosas *acerca de mí*. ¡No puedo más *con ella*!	We're always having problems *with them*. What would they do *without us*? I've nothing *against him*, but Mrs. Pérez said certain things *about me in front of you*. I can't cope *with her* any more!

(ii) **Conmigo, contigo**

There are special forms **conmigo** and **contigo** meaning *with me*, *with you*. See also **consigo** [▶23f(iv)].

El señor Pérez conoce el problema y quiere hablar *contigo*.	Mr. Pérez is aware of the problem and would like to talk *with you*.

–Bueno, hablo *con él*, pero si aquella mujer quiere cenar *conmigo*, tiene que disculparse.	–O.K., I'll speak *to (with) him*, but if that woman wants to have dinner *with me*, she's got to apologize.

(iii) Ello

The neuter form **ello** refers to an idea, or to what has been said.

No quiero hablar más de *ello*.	I don't want to talk about *it* any more.

(iv) Sí

There is also a third person reflexive [➤23c(i)] disjunctive pronoun **sí**, which means *him/herself, oneself, themselves, yourself/selves* (**Vd/Vds**). It is used after prepositions when the object of the preposition is the same as the subject. With **con** (with), the form is **consigo**. This pronoun is often used with **mismo** (self).

Lo hizo para *ella*.	She did it for *her* (i.e. someone else).
Lo hizo para *sí (misma)*.	She did it for *herself*.
Lo trajo consigo.	She brought it with her.

(v)

Certain prepositional phrases are followed by the subject pronoun.

excepto yo	except (for) me
menos yo	except (for) me
entre tú y yo	between you and me

Disjunctive pronouns are sometimes used after **de** to clarify possession [➤21g(v)] or after **a** to emphasize object pronouns [➤8h(v), 23b(ii), (iii)]. They are also used when a verb takes a prepositional object [➤8i].

No *se la* voy a prestar *a él*.	I'm not going to lend it *to him*.

23g *Which one?: interrogative pronouns*

These are the question words listed in paragraphs 6d(i) to 6d(iii).

In Spanish *all* interrogative pronouns have an accent on the stressed vowel.

(i) *¿Quién/quiénes? Who? Whom?*

• **¿Quién?** is used for *who?, whom?*, as subject, object and after a preposition. The plural **quiénes** is used if more than one person is being asked about. When they are the direct object, they are preceded by the personal **a** [➤8e]. The preposition must *always precede* **quién(es)**, and may not come at the end of the clause as often happens in English.

¿Quién **hizo esto?** *¿Quiénes* **hicieron esto?**	*Who* did this?
¿A quién/quiénes **viste?**	*Whom* did you see?
¿Con quién/quiénes **fuiste?**	*Who* did you go *with*? / *With whom* did you go?
¿Para quién/quiénes **lo hicieron?**	*Who* did they do it *for*? / *For whom* did they do it?

• **¿De quién/quiénes...?** Whose?

¿De quién **es este bolso?** *De quiénes* **son estas maletas?**	*Whose* is this bag? *Whose* are these suitcases?

Do not confuse this with the word **cuyo** meaning 'whose', which is a relative pronoun and is not used to ask questions [➤23k(vii)].

(ii) *¿Qué? What?*

¿Qué? is used for *what? what sort of?* [➤23g(iii)], as subject, object or after a preposition (which must precede it).

¿Qué **ha ocurrido?**	*What* has happened?
¿Qué **vio Vd?**	*What* did you see?
¿Con qué **lo hicieron?**	*What* did they do it *with*?
¿Para qué **lo hicieron?**	*What* did they do it *for*?

(iii)   *¿Cuál/cuáles? Which one(s)?*

¿**Cuál?** usually means *which one* and the plural ¿**cuáles?** *which ones?*

Hay varias maletas aquí. *¿Cuál* es de Vd? *¿Cuáles* son de Vd?	There are several suitcases here. *Which (one)* is yours? *Which (ones)* are yours?

Cuál also means *what* in sentences such as *what is the...?*

¿Cuál es la razón del retraso? *¿Cuál es el* mejor vuelo para Bogotá?	*What is the* reason for the delay? *What/which is the* best flight for Bogotá?

For ¿**Qué hora es?** (What is the time?) see paragraph 29b.

23h   *Pointing and showing: demonstrative pronouns*

Demonstrative pronouns refer to something very specific, usually indicating whether it is near to or far from the speaker in time or place. Sometimes this distance is mental rather than physical.

(i)   *Forms*

The demonstrative pronouns take the same forms as the demonstrative determiners [➤21d], where the difference between **este** (this), **ese** (that by you) and **aquel** (that over there) and the agreement in gender and number are fully explained. The pronouns mean *this (one), these (ones), that (one), those (ones)*. It has been traditional to put an accent on the stressed syllable of the pronoun form to distinguish it from the adjective, but the Spanish Academy's *Nuevas normas* (1959) stated that this was not necessary. We have put them on, as many people do continue to do so, but it is not a question over which the learner of Spanish should lose sleep!

Cuál de estas maletas es de Vd: *¿ésta, ésa* o *aquélla?*	Which of these suitcases is yours: *this one, that one* (by you) or *that one* (over there)?
Creo que *aquéllas* son mías.	I think *those* (over there) are mine.

(ii)   *Eso, esto, aquello*

One place where the demonstrative pronoun does differ from the adjective is in having a *neuter* form which is used to refer to an idea or concept which does not have a gender, or to an object which has not been named and therefore cannot yet be given a gender.

Perder mi equipaje – *eso* **siempre me preocupa.**	Losing my luggage – *that* always concerns me.
¿Qué es *esto***?**	What's *this*?

(iii)   *Aquél, éste* the former, the latter

Aquél and **éste** are also used to mean *the former* and *the latter*.

De las dos ciudades, Caracas y Bogotá, *aquélla* **me gusta más que** *ésta*.	Of the two cities, Caracas and Bogotá, I like *the former* more than *the latter*.

23i   *How much? How many?: pronouns of quantity*

Some *quantifiers* refer to the whole or none of something, others to some part or some members of it.

(i)   *Quantifier pronouns*

The following are the *quantifier pronouns* in Spanish. Many resemble closely the quantifier determiners [➤21f].

algo	something, anything
nada	nothing, not...anything
alguien	someone, somebody, anyone, anybody
nadie	no one, nobody, not...anyone/anybody
alguno	one or other; (*plural*) some, a few
ninguno	none, not one, not any
unos	some
cualquiera	any, anyone
todo	all, everything
todos	all, everybody (+ *plural verb*)
todo el mundo	everybody (+ *singular verb*)
todo lo que	all that, everything which
todos los que	all (those) who, all (those) which
cada uno	each one, every one

ambos	both
mucho	a lot, much
muchos	a lot, many
más	more
menos	less
demasiado	too much
demasiados	too many
bastante	enough
varios	several
un poco (de)	a little (of), a bit (of)
poco	little, not much
pocos	few, not many

¿Quiere Vd *algo*? –No, *no* quiero *nada*.	Do you want *something*? –No, I *don't* want *anything*.
¿Hay *alguien* allí? –No, *no* hay *nadie*.	Is there *anyone* there? –No, there's *no one*.
¿Queda *algún vaso* de vino? –No, *no* queda *ninguno*.	Is there *a glass of* wine left? –No, there's *none* left.
Cualquiera ve que tenemos sed, aunque *nadie* lo crea.	*Anyone* can see that we are thirsty, although *no one* believes it.
Mire en *alguna* de las alacenas. Debe de haber *alguno*.	Look in *one or other* of the cabinets. There must be *some*.
Todos han bebido *demasiado*.	You have *all* drunk *too much*.
Hay un pequeño vaso para *cada uno*.	There is a small glass *each (for each one)*.
Pedro y Pablo *no* tienen *ninguno*. No se preocupen, hay *bastante* para *ambos*.	Pedro and Pablo *haven't any*. Don't worry, there's *enough* for *both*.
Todo lo que queda es para ellos.	*All that* is left is for them.

(ii) Negative pronouns

Negative pronouns such as **nada**, **nadie** and **ninguno** need **no** before the verb when they follow it [►27a(ii)] but not when they precede it. **No** is not needed when the verb is preceded by **sin**.

Se fueron *sin dejar nada*.	They went *without leaving anything*.

(iii) Anyone

Care should be taken with the equivalent of *anyone*. *Not...anyone* is, of course, the same as *no one*: **nadie**. *Someone* and *anyone* in the sense *Is anyone/someone there?*, although different in English, are both **alguien** in Spanish. However, *anyone* in the very wide sense of *anyone at all* is **cualquiera**: **cualquiera lo sabe** (anyone knows that). Note that *anyone who...* is **el que...** or **quien...** and is dealt with under *Relative pronouns* in 23k(viii).

(iv) Todo lo que

In a relative clause, *everything which, all that* is **todo lo que** and *all those who/which* is **todos los que/todas las que** [➤23k(viii)].

(v) Mucho(s) de

As pronouns, *a lot of, much/many of* are **mucho de**, **muchos de**.

Mucho del vino ha desaparecido.	*Much of* the wine has disappeared.

Mucho as an adjective is not followed by **de**.

Han bebido *muchas botellas*.	They have drunk *a lot of (many) bottles*.

23j Belonging together: possessive pronouns

Possessive pronouns are unique in that they represent two different nouns at once: the possessor and the thing possessed. Like possessive determiners, they take their *form* from the *possessor*, and their *gender and number* from the *thing possessed*. Take care not to confuse the two: one person can own several things, and several people can be joint owners of one thing.

 It is important to remember in Spanish that the third person pronoun **suyo** can mean not only 'his', 'hers', 'theirs', but also 'yours', belonging to **Vd** or **Vds** [➤23b].

The possessive pronouns are:

el mío	la mía	los míos	las mías	mine
el tuyo	la tuya	los tuyos	las tuyas	yours (**tú**)
el suyo	la suya	los suyos	las suyas	yours (**Vd**)
el suyo	la suya	los suyos	las suyas	his, hers

el nuestro	la nuestra	los nuestros	las nuestras	ours
el vuestro	la vuestra	los vuestros	las vuestras	yours (**vosotros**)
el suyo	la suya	los suyos	las suyas	yours (**Vds**)
el suyo	la suya	los suyos	las suyas	theirs

(i) Use

They are used with the definite article when they replace a noun.

He encontrado *nuestras maletas,* pero no encuentro *las suyas.* *La mía* es gris con correa.	I've found *our suitcases*, but I can't find *yours*. *Mine* is gray with a strap.

(ii) Ambiguity

Where there is ambiguity as to the meaning of the third person pronoun **el suyo** etc., **de** + the disjunctive pronoun [➤23f] is added, in which case **suyo** is often omitted.

Estas maletas son mías y creo que las otras son *de Vds*, ¿no? Sí, pero ésta no es nuestra. Tiene que ser *de ellos*. He encontrado nuestras maletas, pero no encuentro *las de Vds*.	These suitcases are mine and I think the others are *yours*, aren't they? Yes, but this one isn't ours. It must be *theirs*. I've found our suitcases but I can't find *yours*.

This is the same construction as is used when the possessor is a noun: *that/those of*, where English would normally use *'s* [➤21g].

Mi casa y *la de mi hermano*.	My house and *my brother's*.

23k Relative pronouns

(i) Use

A relative pronoun relates or links a noun to a clause which closely follows it and which defines or comments on it. The noun is known as the *antecedent*, and the clause is a relative clause [➤5b]. If it is capable of changing its form, the relative pronoun takes its number and gender from the antecedent.

In Spanish, in order to use the correct relative pronoun, it is helpful to distinguish between a *descriptive* and a *defining* relative clause.

• A *descriptive* clause simply gives you more information about the antecedent, and is normally separated from it by commas, or a pause in speech.

Mi maleta, *que tenía una etiqueta de «Iberia»,* **estaba en la cinta de equipajes.**	My suitcase, *which had an "Iberia" label,* was on the carousel.

The relative clause describes the suitcase.

• A *defining* clause defines the antecedent, and is usually written without commas or spoken without a pause.

La maleta *que estaba en la cinta de equipajes* **tenía una etiqueta de «Iberia».**	The suitcase *that was on the carousel* had an "Iberia" label.

The relative clause defines the suitcase as *the one that was on the carousel.*

(ii)   Forms

The relative pronouns in Spanish are variously **que, quien/quienes, el que/la que/los que/lo que/las que, el cual/la cual/lo cual/los cuales/las cuales**, just as English has, variously, *who, which, that* or no pronoun at all. In view of this, it is best to examine this construction in the light of the *function* of the pronoun, i.e. is it the subject or object of the relative clause or is it after a preposition? Is the antecedent a person or persons, a thing or things?

(iii)   Pronoun as subject [➤4b]

(A) In a defining clause, **que** is normally used to refer to both persons and things, i.e. it means *who, which, that.*

El señor *que* **me ayudó es peruano.**	The gentleman *who/that* helped me is Peruvian.
La maleta *que* **estaba en la cinta de equipaje era mía.**	The suitcase *which/that* was on the carousel was mine.

(B) Que is also usually used in a descriptive clause, although **quien** is sometimes used to refer to people. **El cual**, etc., may be used referring to people or things, but is very emphatic.

El señor, *que/quien/el cual* **era peruano, me ayudó con el equipaje.**	The gentleman, *who* was a Peruvian, helped me with my luggage.
La maleta, *que/la cual* **tenía una gran etiqueta de «Iberia» no se veía en ninguna parte.**	The suitcase, *which* had a large "Iberia" label, was nowhere to be seen.

(iv)   Pronoun as direct object [►8e]

(A) In a defining clause, **que** is used for *which/that* referring to things, and also to people if no personal **a** [►8e] is used; if a personal **a** is used, the relative pronoun is **al que** or **quien**.

La maleta *que* **traje conmigo es grande y gris.**	The suitcase *which/that* I brought with me is large and gray.
El señor *que/al que/a quien* **conocí en el avión me ayudó con el equipaje.**	The gentleman *whom/that/(no pronoun)* I met on the plane helped me with my luggage.

(B) In a descriptive clause, **que** is used for things and **a quien/al que/al cual** for people.

El señor peruano y su señora, *que/a los que/a quienes* **conocí en el avión, son encantadores.**	The Peruvian gentleman and his wife, *whom* I met on the plane, are charming.

(v)   Pronoun after a preposition [►25]

(A) In a defining clause, a preposition + **el que** is used for things and + **el que** or **quien** for people.

La maleta *de la que* **hablamos ha desaparecido.**	The suitcase *about which* we are talking (we are talking *about*) has disappeared.
El señor *con el que/quien* **hablaba en el avión es muy simpático.**	The gentleman *with whom* I was talking (I was talking *with*) on the plane is very nice.

(B) In a descriptive clause, you also use a preposition + **el que** for things, and + **el que** or **quien** for people. **El cual** may be used for both, especially after *compound* prepositions (those that are joined to the noun with **a** or **de**), but it is perhaps becoming a little stilted in modern Spanish.

La maleta, *delante de la que/de la cual* estaba sentada hace unos momentos, ha desaparecido. El señor peruano, *al lado de quien/del cual* estaba sentada en el avión, es encantador.	The suitcase, *in front of which* I was sitting a few minutes ago, has disappeared. The Peruvian gentleman, *beside whom* I was sitting on the plane, is charming.

En que and **de que** are often used instead of **en el que** and **del que**.

Two things that frequently happen in English are *not allowed* in Spanish:
• You *may not omit* the relative pronoun: 'The *suitcase I brought* with me' must become 'The suitcase *which* I brought with me': **La maleta que traje conmigo**.
• The preposition *must precede* the relative pronoun. It *may not* be placed at the end of the relative clause as in English: 'The gentleman I was travelling *with*' must become 'The gentleman *with whom* I was travelling': **El señor con quien viajaba**.

(vi) *Pronouns referring to an idea or sentence*

When the relative pronoun refers to an idea or a sentence, i.e. not to a noun with a known gender, the neuter pronoun **lo que** or **lo cual** must be used [➤23e(ii)].

La maleta desapareció, *lo que/lo cual* no me gustó nada.	The suitcase disappeared, *which* didn't please me at all.

It wasn't *the suitcase* that didn't please the speaker, but *the fact that it disappeared*.

(vii) **Cuyo**

Cuyo means *whose*, and although it is strictly a determiner, it is convenient to deal with it here. It takes its gender and number from the thing possessed. The antecedent may be a person or a thing.

| El señor, con *cuya* señora estaba hablando, es peruano. | The gentleman, with *whose* wife I was talking, is Peruvian. |
| El aeropuerto, *cuyos* clientes siempre se quejan, no trata de rectificar el problema. | The airport, *whose* customers are always complaining, is not trying to solve the problem. |

(viii) *Those who*

He who, the one who, those who, the ones who, people who, those which, whoever, etc. are usually translated by **el/la/los/las que**. If the antecedent is indefinite as in the last example below, the verb is in the subjunctive [▶16d(i)].

Los que han perdido la maleta tienen que dirigirse a aquella oficina.	*Those who* have lost their suitcases have to apply to that office.
Las que desaparecen suelen reaparecer dentro de unos días.	*Those (i.e.suitcases) which* disappear usually reappear within a few days.
El que crea que va a volver a verla hoy es muy optimista.	*He who/whoever* thinks that he will see it again today is very optimistic.

24 Giving vent to your feelings: exclamations and interjections

24a Exclamations

Exclamations express emotions such as delight, anger, surprise or fear. They are usually introduced by ¡Qué...! *What (a)...!* + a noun phrase, or *How...!* + an adjective or adverb. Very often they are not complete sentences, though it is obvious what the rest of the sentence might be.

¡Qué risa!	What a laugh!/How funny!
¡Qué lástima!	What a pity!/Isn't it a shame!
¡Qué barbaridad!	How shocking!
¡Qué triste!	How sad!
¡Qué vago eres!	How lazy you are!/Aren't you lazy!
¡Qué joven pareces!	How young you look!
¡Qué bien escribe!	How well (s)he writes!

• *How* + adjective or adverb + verb can also be rendered by **lo** [➤23e(ii)] + adjective or adverb + verb. The adjective agrees with the noun it describes.

¡Lo lista que es Anita!	How clever Anita is!
¡Lo rápidamente que trabajas!	How quickly you work!

• The Spanish equivalent of *what a* + adjective + noun is **qué** + adjective + noun in the few cases where the adjective precedes the noun, but **qué** + noun + **tan** or **más** + adjective when the adjective follows.

¡Qué buen hombre!	What a kind man!
¡Qué ciudad tan grande!	What a big city!
¡Qué película más divertida!	What a funny movie!
¡Qué nariz tan roja tienes!	What a red nose you've got!

• *What a lot* is **¡cuánto...!**.

| **¡Cuántos regalos he tenido!** | What a lot of presents I've had! |
| **¡Cuánta gente!** | What a lot of people! |

• *(Just) look how,..!* is **¡cómo!** + verb.

| **¡Cómo nieva!** | Look how it's snowing! |
| **¡Cómo has crecido!** | Just look how you've grown! |

➤ See also **¡ojalá...!** *if only...* in 16e(i).

24b Interjections

Interjections range from words or short phrases which are really cut-down exclamations through standard noises associated with various emotions to whatever may be wrung from you in the heat of the moment.

• Some are reactions to the senses – pain, taste, smell, sound, sight, and are barely words.

¡Ah!	Ah!/Oh!
¡Ay!	Oh!/Ah!/Ouch!/Alas! (general purpose interjection)
¡Huy!	Oh!/Well!/Phew!
¡Puf!	Ugh!/Bah!

• Some express surprise, or disbelief.

¡Caramba!	Wow!
¡Caray!	Wow!
¡Dios mío!	Good heavens!/Well I never!
¡Jesús!	Good heavens!
¡Anda!	Well I never!/Go on!
¡Vaya!	Well, well!
¡No me diga(s)!	You don't say!
¿Verdad?	Really?
¿De veras?	Really?

• Some express pleading or exhortation to action.

¡Por Dios!	For goodness sake!/For heaven's sake!
¡Vamos!	Come on!/Get on with it!
¡Venga!	Come on!

- Some contain a warning or instruction.

¡Cuidado!	Mind!/Watch out!
¡Ojo!	Watch out!
¡Socorro!	Help!
¡Tenga!	Here you are!
¡Chist!	Ssssh! Hush!

- Some express reactions such as indignation, disappointment or disgust.

¡Ni hablar!	No way!/Not on your life!
¡En absoluto!	Not at all!/No way!
¡Ni mucho menos!	Not at all!/Far from it!!
¿Y qué?	So what?
¡Fatal!	Awful!/Dreadful!/Terrible!
¡Mierda!	Hell!/Shit!
¡Puaj!	Yuck!

- Others pleasure or joy.

¡Estupendo!	Super!/Great!
¡Fantástico!	Super!/Great!
¡Ñam ñam!	Yum yum!
¡Olé!	Hurrah!/Hooray!/Bravo!

24c *Spanish invocations and expletives*

(i) *Religious figures*

The invocation of religious figures – **Dios**, **Jesús**, **Jesucristo**, **Cristo**, **la Virgen María** – is not regarded as blasphemous or as 'strong' as it tends to be in English.

(ii) *Sexual terminology*

Spanish swearwords contain a considerable range of sexual terminology which it is beyond a book such as this to impart. As a non-native speaker you are well advised to exercise prudence in their use until you are confident of their acceptability and suitability, and that you will not offend!

E

LINKING AND MODIFYING MEANINGS: PREPOSITIONS AND ADVERBIAL EXPRESSIONS

213

25 Linking noun phrases into the sentence: prepositions

25a What does a preposition do?

A preposition is a connecting word. It links the meaning of the noun phrase which follows it either to the verb or to another noun phrase which comes before it.

25b Prepositional phrases linked to verbs

A prepositional phrase can be linked to a verb in two ways.

(i) Free-standing adverbial expression

The prepositional phrase may be a free-standing adverbial expression [➤27], which modifies or extends the meaning of the verb by answering questions such as **¿Cuándo?** (When?), **¿Dónde?** (Where?) or **¿Cómo?** (How?) [➤6d(vi)–(viii)].

¿Cuándo salieron Vds de casa? –Salimos *a las diez.*	When did you leave home? –We left *at ten o'clock.*
¿Dónde pararon a almorzar? –Paramos *en Córdoba.*	Where did you stop for lunch? –We stopped *in Córdoba.*
¿Cómo viajaron? –Viajamos *en coche.*	How did you travel? –We travelled *by car.*

(ii)

Certain common prepositions link particular verbs to following noun phrases [➤8i] or to the infinitive of another verb [➤8k]. (See the paragraphs mentioned for details.)

25c Prepositional phrases after noun phrases

A prepositional phrase may be linked to a noun phrase in two ways.

(i)

It may do the job of an adjective [➤22b], answering the question **¿Qué...?** (Which...?). It can then be thought of as an abbreviated relative clause.

| En Córdoba tomamos *un bocadillo de jamón* y *una caña de cerveza*. Luego buscamos *gasolina sin plomo*. | In Córdoba we had a *ham sandwich* and a *glass of beer*. Then we looked for some *unleaded gasoline*. |

(ii) Certain nouns, especially those related to the verbs in paragraph 8k, have a similar fixed link with the preposition which connects them to the following noun phrase. However, many nouns are linked with **de**, whatever preposition the corresponding verb takes. The same is true of some adjectives.

Gracias *por* su *ayuda para encontrar* un buen itinerario, aunque tuvimos una verdadera lucha *por encontrar* nuestro camino por Sevilla.	Thanks for your *help in finding* a good route, though we had a real *struggle to find our way* through Seville.
Sus *consejos de tomar* la autopista hasta Sevilla y nuestra *decisión de seguirlos* nos ahorraron bastante tiempo.	Your *advice to take* the highway as far as Seville and our *decision to follow it* saved us quite a lot of time.
¡Somos muy *capaces de errores*!	We are very *capable of mistakes*!

(iii) Possession

There is no equivalent in Spanish of the English *apostrophe s* and the thing possessed is linked to the possessor by the preposition **de** [➤23j(ii)].

| *Los consejos de nuestros amigos* eran muy buenos. *El tráfico de Sevilla* puede ser muy denso. | *Our friends' advice* was very good. *Seville's traffic* can be very heavy. |

25d **Verbs after prepositions**

The only part of the verb which can follow a preposition is the infinitive [➤10a(iv)].

| *Después de salir* de Cádiz tomamos la autopista *sin considerar* otra carretera. | *After leaving* Cádiz we took the highway *without considering* any other road. |

| Al llegar a Córdoba, nos paramos a almorzar. | On arriving at Córdoba, we stopped to have lunch. |

Usually the only personal pronouns which can follow a preposition are the disjunctive or prepositional pronouns [▶23f].

25e Common prepositions

Prepositions in Spanish can be one word or compound prepositions of two or more words joined to the following noun or pronoun with **a** or **de**.

(i) Simple prepositions

a	to (implies motion), at (a time, rate, speed) (no meaning when used as 'personal **a**' [▶8e])
bajo	under, beneath
con	with
contra	against
de	of, from, about (on the subject of)
desde	from, since
durante	during, for (a completed time)
en	in, at (implies position)
entre	between, among
hacia	towards
hasta	as far as, up to, until
mediante	by means of
para	for, in order to [▶25e(iv)]
por	by, through, because of, for [▶25e(v)]
según	according to
sin	without
sobre	on, over, about (on the subject of)
tras	behind, after (mainly in written Spanish)

(ii) Compound prepositions

All of these involve the contractions **al** and **del** [▶21c(iii)] when used with a masculine singular noun.

a causa de	because of
a la derecha de	on the right of
a la izquierda de	on the left of
al final de	at the end of

al lado de	beside, next to
al otro lado de	on the other side of
alrededor de	around
antes de	before
a razón de	because of, owing to
cerca de	near
debajo de	under, beneath
debido a	owing to
delante de	in front of
dentro de	inside, within (*an object or a time*)
después de	after
detrás de	behind
encima de	over, on top of, above
enfrente de	opposite
en lugar de	instead of, in place of
en medio de	in the middle/midst of
en torno a	around
en vez de	instead of, in place of
frente a	opposite, faced with
fuera de	outside, away from
gracias a	thanks to
Junto a	next to
(no) lejos de	(not) far/a long way from
por medio de	by means of

(iii)   *Para and por*

These two prepositions are frequently confused by learners of Spanish. Basically **para** indicates purpose: **¿Para qué?** means *What for?, For what purpose?* and **por** indicates cause: **¿Por qué?** means *Why?, For what reason?*.

(iv)   *Para*

Para usually means:

(A) *For*, in the sense *destined for*, *intended for*, *considering*.

En Córdoba compramos unas flores *para la tía María. Para un hombre* no escogí mal, ¿verdad?	In Córdoba we bought some flowers *for Aunt Mary. For a man*, I didn't choose badly, did I?

(B) *By* a certain time or *for the duration of* a certain time in the future.

La semana que viene vamos a Francia *para quince días*.	Next week we are going to France *for two weeks*.
Las flores estarán listas *para las tres*.	The flowers will be ready *for/by* three o'clock.

(C) *In order to* + infinitive.

***Para encontrar* un florista tuvimos que ir al mercado.**	*(In order) to find* a florist we had to go to the market.

(v)   Por

Por usually means:

(A) *By*, expressing the agent or instrument of a passive verb [➤17d].

Estas flores son cultivadas *por* una empresa de horticultores de la comarca.	These flowers are grown *by* a firm of local growers.

(B) *For* meaning *through*, *because of*, *as a result of*.

La empresa es famosa *por* sus geranios, pero no pudimos visitarla *por* la necesidad de continuar nuestro viaje.	The firm is famous *for* its geraniums, but we couldn't visit it *because of* the need to continue our journey.

(C) *For* meaning *in exchange for*.

Gracias *por* las flores. Has debido pagar bastante *por* ellas.	Thanks *for* the flowers. You must have paid a lot *for* them.

(D) *Through, via, along*.

Salimos *por* Sevilla, luego pasamos *por* el río.	We set out *through* Seville, then we went *along* the river.

(E) Motion *around*, or *all over*, sometimes linking with other prepositions.

Dimos un paseo *por* las calles de la ciudad. Luego subimos *por* la rampa hasta lo alto de la Giralda. Desde allí vimos toda la ciudad *por debajo de* nosotros.	We took a walk *around* the streets of the city. Then we went up *by* the ramp to the top of the Giralda. From there we could see all the city *below* us.

(F) *For* a completed period of time, usually in the past.

Nos quedamos allí *por* media hora.	We stayed there *for* half an hour.

(G) It is also used in the following common adverbial phrases:

por la mañana	in the morning
por la tarde	in the afternoon
por la noche	at night
por ahora	for now
por si acaso	just in case

and many others.

 Para **siempre** forever

26 Types of adverbial expression

26a What is an adverbial expression?

Adverbial expressions (often shortened to *adverbials*) mainly answer the questions listed in paragraphs 6d(vi) to 6d(x). We say that they modify meanings because they complete, alter or even contradict them. They may modify the meanings of verbs, of adjectives or of the whole sentence. There are three sorts of adverbial: adverbs, adverbial phrases and adverbial clauses. They all play the same part in the sentence – you can often say the same thing using any one of them.

| **antes** | **antes de la reunión** | **antes de que empezara la reunión** |
| before | before the meeting | before the meeting started |

26b Adverbs

These are single word expressions, of two types.

(i) Adverbs formed from adjectives [➤22]

Most of these adverbs answer the question **¿Cómo?** (How?), though they can answer other questions.

Just as English adverbs are formed by adding '-ly' to the adjective, Spanish adverbs are formed by adding **-mente** to the feminine singular of the adjective [➤22a].

Adjective	*Feminine singular*	*Adverb*	
rápido	**rápida**	**rápidamente**	quickly
sincero	**sincera**	**sinceramente**	sincerely
principal	**principal**	**principalmente**	principally
reciente	**reciente**	**recientemente**	recently

• The adverbs from **bueno** (good) and **malo** (bad) are **bien** (well) and **mal** (badly) respectively.

• Any stress accent remains as on the original adjective.

• When there would be two or more adverbs ending in **-mente** used consecutively, the adjectives are in the feminine form where applicable but **-mente** is only added to the last one.

Se avanzaban *lenta, cautelosa y silenciosamente.*	They were advancing *slowly, cautiously and silently.*

- Devices for avoiding long adverbs.

(A) As the addition of **-mente** makes some adverbs rather long and clumsy, Spanish often converts the adverb to an adverbial phrase [➤26c] using **con** or another suitable preposition + noun or **de un modo** (*masculine*)/**de una manera** (*fominine*) + adjective [➤20b, 22a, 26c].

Se avanzaban *con lentitud y cautela y en silencio.* Se avanzaban *de un modo lento, cauteloso y silencioso.* Se avanzaban *de una manera lenta, cautelosa y silenciosa.*	They were advancing *slowly, cautiously and silently.*

(B) In formal style, use the adjective which agrees with the subject of the verb [➤22c(i)].

Se avanzaban *lentos, cautelosos y silenciosos.*	They were advancing *slowly, cautiously and silently.*

(ii) *Other adverbs*

Many of the most common adverbs, especially answering the questions ¿**Cuándo?** (When?) and ¿**Dónde?** (Where?), are not formed from adjectives. These are listed, together with common adverbial phrases, in chapter 27.

(iii) *'More' and 'most'*

Most adverbs made from adjectives can be used to make comparisons: for this we use the comparative form. If we are comparing the actions of more than two people or things, then we use the superlative.

- The comparative of adverbs in Spanish is formed in the same way as for adjectives [➤22d(i)]: you simply put **más** (more) before the adverb and **que** (than) after it if necessary.

Vds habrán ido a un concierto *más recientemente que* nosotros.	You will have been to a concert *more recently than* we have.

- In most cases, the superlative [►22d(ii)] of the adverb is the same as the comparative.

Son nuestros amigos los que han ido *más recientemente* a un concierto.	It's our friends who have been *most recently* to a concert.

- The comparative and superlative of **bien** (well) is **mejor** (better, best) and of **mal** (badly) is **peor** (worse, worst).

Esta es la orquesta que toca *mejor*.	This is the orchestra which plays *best*.

- The negative comparative with **menos** (less, least) works in the same way.

Vds pueden ir a los conciertos *menos fácilmente que* nosotros. Son nuestros vecinos los que pueden ir a los conciertos *menos fácilmente*.	You can get to concerts *less easily than* we can. It's our neighbors who can get to concerts *the least easily*.

- The 'comparison of equality' is formed with **(no) tan...como** ([not] so...as) or with **tanto como** (as much, as many...as) [►22d(iv)].

Vds van a conciertos *tan frecuentemente como* nosotros. A Vds les gustan los conciertos *tanto como* a nosotros.	You go to concerts *as frequently as* we do. You enjoy concerts *as much as* we do.

- It is possible to add **-mente** to the superlative form of the adjective ending in **-ísimo**, meaning *extremely*, *very, very* [►22d(v)] to form an adverb.

Si queremos ir a este concierto hay que actuar *rapidísimamente*.	If we want to go to this concert we must act *very quickly*.

26c   Adverbial phrases

Sometimes a noun phrase [➤20b] acts as an adverbial, as in **Habla *todo el tiempo*** (He talks *all the time*), but most adverbial phrases begin with a preposition. They are discussed in chapter 27. We have already noted above [➤26b(i)] that in Spanish you often use a noun phrase beginning with a preposition in preference to a long adverb ending in **-mente**.

Hay un gran número de conciertos *en la capital*. Los mejores se dan *con frecuencia en la sala de conciertos a orillas del río cerca del puente*.	There are a great number of concerts *in the capital*. The best are *often* given *in the concert hall on the river bank near the bridge*.

26d   Adverbial clauses

Unlike the phrases, adverbial clauses contain a main verb and are introduced by a subordinating conjunction. These clauses are discussed in paragraph 5a(ii). Many have the verb in the subjunctive [➤16c].

Quisiéramos ir a aquel concierto *porque la orquesta es muy famosa*.	We would like to go to that concert *because the orchestra is very famous*.
Quisiéramos ir, *aunque las entradas sean bastante caras*.	We would like to go, *even if the tickets are quite expensive*.
Si vamos a conseguir entradas, tendremos que sacarlas cuanto antes.	*If we are going to get tickets*, we shall have to get them as soon as possible.

27 What adverbial expressions do

27a Negative expressions

(i) Making a verb negative

To make a verb negative, **no** is placed immediately before it, and can only be separated from it by object pronouns [➤23b, c].

No tengo mi monedero. ¡No lo tengo!	I *don't have/haven't got* my purse. I *don't have/haven't got* it!

(ii)

If a negative expression follows the verb in Spanish, **no** must be placed before the verb; if the negative expression comes first, or there is no verb, or the verb is preceded by **sin** (without), **no** is not required.

Most, though not all, negative expressions are adverbials, and it is convenient to list all of them here, since the above rule applies to them all.

no	not
nunca	never, not ever
jamás	never, not ever
en mi vida	never in my life
de ninguna manera	no way, not in any way
de ningún modo	no way, not in any way
en ninguna parte	nowhere, not anywhere
en ningún sitio	nowhere, not anywhere
tampoco	neither, not either (*negative of* **también** (also))
ni...ni....	neither...nor...
ni	nor
ya no	no more, no longer

and also the pronouns [➤23i(i)]

nada	nothing, not anything	**nadie**	nobody, not anybody

and the determiner [➤21f(ii)].

ninguno	no, not any

En mi vida he entendido por qué los miembros de una orquesta llevan negro.	*Never in my life* have I understood why members of an orchestra wear black.
¡No he visto en ninguna parte una orquesta que se vista de amarillo!	*I haven't seen* an orchestra dressed in yellow *anywhere*!
¡Ni en rojo *tampoco*! (¡*Tampoco* en rojo!)	*Nor* in red *either*!
Sin haber pensado *nunca* en esto, ¡tengo que admitir que es verdad!	*Without ever* having thought about it, I have to admit that it's true!

27b   Other adverbs and adverbial phrases

These answer various questions.

(i)   ¿Cuándo? When?: time [➤6d(vi)]

ahora	now
a menudo	often
anoche	last night, yesterday evening
antes	before, beforehand
anteayer	the day before yesterday
ayer	yesterday
actualmente	at the present time
ahora mismo	right now
a tiempo	on time
algunas veces	sometimes
a veces	sometimes
muchas veces	often
rara vez	seldom
una vez	once
con frecuencia	frequently, often
después	after, afterwards
el domingo por la tarde	(on) Sunday afternoon
en seguida	at once, straightaway, right away
entonces	then, at that time
luego	then, next
mañana	tomorrow
mañana por la mañana	tomorrow morning
mañana por la tarde	tomorrow afternoon
mañana por la noche	tomorrow night

nunca	never
pasado mañana	the day after tomorrow
pronto	soon
por ahora	for now
por el momento	for the moment, for the present
los sábados por la noche	(on) Saturday nights
temprano	early
tarde	late
más tarde	later
de aquí en adelante	henceforth, from now on
siempre	always
ya	already, now

Anoche fuimos a un concierto y *después* cenamos en un restaurante. *Mañana* vamos a ir a otro. Viviendo en el campo *nunca* vamos a conciertos, y se olvida *pronto* que *siempre* hay buenos conciertos en la capital.

Last night we went to a concert and *afterwards* we had dinner in a restaurant. Tomorrow we're going to another one. Living in the country we *never* go to concerts, and one *soon* forgets that there are *always* good concerts in the capital.

Actualmente los hombres llevan *a veces* chaqueta blanca, pero *por el momento* nada va a cambiar.

At the present time the men *sometimes* wear a white jacket, but *for the moment* nothing is going to change.

(ii)   *¿Cómo? How?: manner, methods and means [➤6d(viii)]*

a propósito	on purpose, by the way
así	thus, so, like that
asimismo	likewise
bien	well
de espaldas	with one's back to
de puntillas	on tiptoe
del mismo modo	in the same way
de la misma manera	in the same way
demasiado	too, too much
de repente	suddenly
de soslayo	askance, obliquely
en autobús	by bus
en avión	by plane
en bicicleta	by bicycle

en (el) tren	by train
entonces	then, at that time
mal	badly
por desgracia	unfortunately

> *A propósito*, **creo reconocer a un amigo en el concierto, pero no le veía *bien*, porque *por desgracia* estaba *de espaldas*.**
>
> *By the way,* I thought I recognized a friend at the concert, but I couldn't see him *well*, because *unfortunately* he was standing *with his back to me.*

(iii)   ¿Dónde? Where?: place [▶6d(vii)]

acá	here, to here (*Spanish American*)
aquí	here
ahí	there (by you)
allí	there (over there) [▶21d, 23h]
allá	there (way over there)
delante	in front
adelante	forwards, henceforth
dentro	inside, within
adentro	(to) inside (*with motion*)
detrás	behind
atrás	backwards
encima	above, on top
fuera	outside, out
afuera	(to) outside (*with motion*)
en alguna parte	somewhere
en cualquier parte	anywhere
en ninguna parte	nowhere
en otra parte	elsewhere, somewhere else
en todas partes	everywhere

(**A** replaces **en** if motion is involved.)

debajo	underneath, beneath, below
abajo	down, below, down below, down with...!, downstairs
arriba	above, upstairs
allí abajo	down there
allí arriba	up there

calle abajo	down the street
calle arriba	up the street
río abajo	downstream
río arriba	upstream

¿Dónde quieres sentarte? ¿Aquí, ahí o allí? Prefiero sentarme *delante*, no me gusta tener el balcón *encima*. ¡Hace más calor *dentro* que *fuera*!

Where do you want to sit? *Here, there (where you are)* or *over there*? I prefer to sit in *front*. I don't like having the balcony *above me*. It's warmer *inside* than *out*!

- Some common adverbs of place are in fact adverbial phrases in Spanish [➤26c].

en todas partes everywhere   **en ninguna parte** nowhere

Dejé el programa del concierto *en alguna parte*, pero no lo veo *en ninguna parte*. He buscado *en todas partes*. Tiene que estar *arriba*.

I left the concert program *somewhere*, but I can't find it *anywhere*. I've looked *everywhere*. It must be *upstairs*.

- A number of these adverbs can be made into compound prepositions linked to a noun by **de** (**delante de**, in front of) [➤25e(ii)].

(iv)   ¿*Cuánto?* How much?: degree [➤6d(ix)]

bastante	enough, a lot, quite a lot
mucho	a lot, much, a great deal
muchísimo	very much, a very great deal
poco	little, not much
poquísimo	very little
un poco	a little, a bit
más	more
menos	less
cada vez más	more and more
cada vez menos	less and less
todo	all, completely

| Claro que me preocupa *bastante*. En efecto, me preocupa *cada vez más*. | Of course it worries me *a lot*. In fact, it worries me *more and more*. |

(v)   *¿Por qué?* Why?: reasons [➤6d(x)]

| **por lo tanto** | therefore | **entonces** | then, therefore |

| *Por lo tanto* voy a seguir buscándolo *entonces*. | *So* I'm going to go on looking for it *then*. |

27c   *The order of adverbials in the sentence*

There is no absolute hard-and-fast rule in Spanish about the position and order of adverbials in the sentence, though the following observations may be helpful in addition to the general observations on word order [➤4g].

• Adverbials usually occur *immediately before* or *immediately after* the word they modify, and those of *time* usually occur before those of *place*.

| La orquesta tocaba *otra vez* la abertura 1812 cuando *al sonar los cañones desde el balcón* gritaron «bravo». | The orchestra was playing the 1812 Overture *again*, when *at the sound of the cannons* they shouted "bravo" *from the balcony*. |

• Adverbials of manner tend to be placed immediately after intransitive verbs [➤8b], but after the complete verb phrase when the verb is transitive.

| Esta orquesta tocó *estupendamente* anoche. La orquesta tocó la abertura *estupendamente* anoche. | This orchestra played *superbly* last night. The orchestra played the overture *superbly* last night. |

- Like other parts of speech, adverbials may be placed early in the sentence for emphasis.

Anoche **la orquesta tocó estupendamente.**	*Last night* the orchestra played superbly.

F
USING NUMBERS

 **Numerals**

28a   Counting: cardinal numbers

1	uno (un/una)	40	cuarenta
2	dos	41	cuarenta y uno (un/una)
3	tres	42	cuarenta y dos, etc.
4	cuatro		
5	cinco	50	cincuenta
6	seis	60	sesenta
7	siete	70	setenta
8	ocho	80	ochenta
9	nueve	90	noventa
10	diez	100	cien
11	once	101	ciento uno (un/una)
12	doce	102	ciento dos
13	trece	110	ciento diez
14	catorce	125	ciento veinticinco
15	quince	199	ciento noventa
16	dieciséis		y nueve
17	diecisiete		
18	dieciocho	200	doscientos/doscientas
19	diecinueve	201	doscientos uno/un,
20	veinte		doscientas una
21	veintiuno	258	doscientos/as
	(veintiún/veintiuna)		cincuenta y ocho
22	veintidós	300	trescientos/as
23	veintitrés	400	cuatrocientos/as
24	veinticuatro	500	quinientos/as
25	veinticinco	600	seiscientos/as
26	veintiséis	700	setecientos/as
27	veintisiete	800	ochocientos/as
28	veintiocho	900	novecientos/as
29	veintinueve	999	novecientos/as noventa
			y nueve
30	treinta		
31	treinta y uno (un/una)	1.000	mil
32	treinta y dos, etc.	1.005	mil cinco

1.588	mil quinientos/as ochenta y ocho	100.000	cien mil
1.995	mil novecientos noventa y cinco	1.000.000	un millón
		2.000.000	dos millones
2.000	dos mil	3.456.789	tres millones, cuatrocientos cincuenta y seis mil, setecientos ochenta y nueve
3.000	tres mil		
20.000	veinte mil		
85.000	ochenta y cinco mil		

As can be seen from the above table, the cardinal numbers in Spanish are fairly straightforward, though the following points should be borne in mind.

(A) Uno is the full masculine form of *one* and is used when no noun follows it. Before a masculine noun it contracts to **un** and becomes **una** when referring to a feminine noun (**un** before a stressed **a-** or **ha-** [▶21e(i)]). This happens with *any* number ending in **-uno**.

Hay *treinta y un hombres* y *cuarenta y una mujeres* en el grupo.	There are *thirty-one men* and *forty-one women* in the group.
¿Cuántos hombres? *–Treinta y uno.* –¿Y cuántas mujeres? *–Cuarenta y una.*	How many men? *–Thirty-one.* –And how many women? *–Forty-one.*

(B) Up to 30, numbers are written as one word. Note the need for a stress accent on **dieciséis** (16), the shortened form **veintiún** (21), **veintidós** (22), **veintitrés** (23) and **veintiséis** (26) [▶2c(i)].

(C) From 31 to 99 **y** is used between tens and units, and the numbers are written as separate words. **Y** is *never* placed between hundreds and tens as *and* is in English.

(D) When 100 stands by itself or before a noun, it is **cien**; when another number follows it, i.e. when you say *a hundred and something,* it is **ciento**.

¿Cuántas personas hay? *–Cien.* Hay *cien personas.* No, perdón, hay *ciento dos.*	How many people are there? *–A hundred.* There are *a hundred people.* No, sorry, there are *a hundred and two.*

(E) The expressions for 200 to 900 are one word ending in -os, which changes to -as when qualifying a feminine noun: this is a frequent occurrence in Spanish-speaking countries where the currency, e.g. the Spanish peseta, is feminine.

¿Cuánto vale? *–Seiscientas* **pesetas.**	How much is it? *–Six hundred pesetas.*

(F) The words for 500, 700 and 900 are **quini**entos, **sete**cien-tos and **nove**cientos.

(G) The word for 1,000, **mil**, is not made plural in a number: **dos mil** (two thousand), although you can say **miles de** (thousands of).

¡Hay *miles de* **palabras en un idioma como el español!**	There are *thousands of* words in a language like Spanish!

(H) *A million* is **un millón**, *two million* **dos millones**, etc. They are linked to a following noun by **de**.

Madrid tiene *tres millones de* **habitantes.**	Madrid has *three million* inhabitants.

(I) In Spain, a dot is used between thousands and a comma to separate decimal points, in common with continental European practice. In some parts of Spanish-speaking America, US and UK practice (i.e. the reverse) is sometimes followed.

2.867	**dos mil ochocientos**	two thousand eight
	sesenta y siete	hundred and sixty-seven
2,867	**dos coma ocho, seis, siete**	two point eight six seven

28b   *Arranging in order: ordinal numbers*

(i)   The ordinal numbers – **primero** (first), etc. – are adjectives and must agree in gender and number with the noun(s) they qualify.

Primero and **tercero** shorten to **primer** and **tercer** before a masculine singular noun [➤22b(i)].

El *primer* hombre está en el
tercer asiento.

The *first* man is in the *third* seat.

(ii)   The only commonly used ordinal numbers are:

primero	first	**sexto**	sixth
segundo	second	**sé(p)timo**	seventh
tercero	third	**octavo**	eighth
cuarto	fourth	**noveno**	ninth
quinto	fifth	**décimo**	tenth

and occasionally

centésimo	hundredth	**milésimo**	thousandth

(iii)   Although ordinals do exist for other numbers (**duodécimo**, 12th; **décimoquinto**, 15th, etc.) they are seldom used. Cardinal numbers are generally used in their place, especially with monarchs, Popes, anniversaries, birthdays, etc.

Alfonso *Décimo*, «el Sabio», reinó en el siglo *trece*.
Alfonso *Trece* abdicó en 1931.
El rey actual de España es Juan Carlos *Primero*. En 1988 celebró su *cincuenta* cumpleaños.

Alfonso *the Tenth*, "The Wise", reigned in the *thirteenth* century. Alfonso *the Thirteenth* abdicated in 1931. The present king of Spain is Juan Carlos *the First*. In 1988 he celebrated his *fiftieth* birthday.

28c   *Sharing out: fractions*

1/2	un medio	1/4	un cuarto
1/3	un tercio	1/5	un quinto

and so on, using the ordinals [➤26b above] up to:

1/10   un décimo

From **once** (11) upwards, add **-avo** to the cardinal number.

1/11	un onceavo	1/100	un centavo/
1/16	un dieciseisavo, *etc.*		centésimo

• Most of these fraction forms are only used in mathematics; in non-specialist contexts, phrases such as **una tercera parte**, **la sexta parte** are preferred.

> **Las dos terceras partes del mundo están debajo del agua.**
> Two-thirds of the world is under water.

- *Half* of a specific object or concept is **la mitad**.

> **¿Quieres la mitad de mi naranja?**
> Would you like *half* (of) my orange?

28d   Grouping and estimating: collective numbers

Spanish has a few collective numbers which are useful for giving an approximate number. They are all joined to the following noun by **de**.

un par (de)	a couple (of), a pair (of)
una decena (de)	about ten (of)
una docena (de)	a dozen (of)
una quincena (de)	about fifteen (of), about two weeks, a fortnight
una veintena (de)	about twenty (of)
un centenar (de)	about a hundred (of)
centenares/cientos (de)	hundreds of
un millar (de)	about a thousand (of)
millares/miles (de)	thousands (of)
millones (de)	millions (of)

> **Había *centenares de personas* allí y tuvimos que esperar *un par de horas*.**
> There were *hundreds of people* there and we had to wait *a couple of hours*.

Telling the time

29a   Giving the time

In Spanish, as in English, there are two ways of giving the time: the conversational way (**las siete menos cuarto**, a quarter of/to seven) and the timetable or digital way (**las seis cuarenta y cinco**, **las dieciocho cuarenta y cinco**, six forty-five, eighteen forty-five).

29b   Time phrases

The Spanish for *What is the time?* is **¿Qué hora es?** and *Have you the time, please?* is **¿Tiene (Vd) la hora, por favor?**.

Es la una	It's one o'clock
Son las dos	It's two o'clock
Son las siete	It's seven o'clock
Es la una y diez	It's ten after/past one, one-ten
Son las cuatro y cuarto	It's a quarter after/past four
Son las cuatro quince	It's four-fifteen
Son las seis y media	It's half past six
Son las seis treinta	It's six-thirty
Son las nueve menos cuarto	It's a quarter of/to nine
Son las ocho cuarenta y cinco	It's eight forty-five
Son las once menos cinco	It's five of/to eleven
Son las diez cincuenta y cinco	It's ten fifty-five

• When **la una** (one o'clock) is mentioned, the verb is singular, but with all other hours it is plural. **Ser** [▶8d(i)] is the verb usually used in expressing the time, but **dar** can be used, meaning *strike*.

Daban las doce **cuando volvimos a casa.**	*It was striking twelve* when we came home.

• *At* a particular time is **a la(s)**...

> *A qué hora* sale el avión? –Sale
> *a las diez y media.*
>
> *At what time* does the plane
> leave? –It leaves *at half-past ten.*

* A.M. and P.M. are expressed by **de la mañana, de la tarde** or **de la noche** or in official business (timetables, opening and closing times, etc.) by using the 24 hour clock.

> **El avión sale a las diez y media**
> **de la noche.**
> **El avión sale a las** *veintidós*
> **treinta.**
>
> The plane leaves at half past ten
> P.M. *(at night).*
> The plane leaves at *twenty-two*
> *thirty.*

* *At about* a time is **sobre** or **a eso de**. *By* a time is **para** [▶25e(iv)].

> **Saldremos de casa** *sobre/a eso*
> *de* **las nueve y llegaremos al**
> **aeropuerto** *para* **las nueve y**
> **media.**
>
> We'll leave home *about nine* and
> get to the airport *by* half past nine.

mediodía   noon, midday   **medianoche**   midnight

 The calendar

Days and months in Spanish are not spelled with a capital letter [►2c(vi)].

30a   Days of the week

lunes	Monday	**viernes**	Friday
martes	Tuesday	**sábado**	Saturday
miércoles	Wednesday	**domingo**	Sunday
jueves	Thursday		

'On Thursday' is **el jueves**, 'on Thursdays' is **los jueves** [►21c(v)].

Note also:

el viernes que viene	next Friday, this coming Friday
el viernes próximo	next Friday
el sábado pasado	last Saturday
el sábado anterior	the Saturday before
el domingo por la mañana	(on) Sunday morning
el martes por la tarde	(on) Tuesday afternoon
los lunes por la noche	(on) Monday nights

30b   Months of the year

enero	January	**julio**	July
febrero	February	**agosto**	August
marzo	March	**se(p)tiembre**	September
abril	April	**octubre**	October
mayo	May	**noviembre**	November
junio	June	**diciembre**	December

Vamos a Caracas *en enero*.	We're going to Caracas *in January*.

30c   Dates

From the 2nd to the 31st of the month, the cardinal numbers [►28a] followed by **de** are used to express the date.

| El dos de febrero y el treinta y uno de marzo. | The second of February and the thirty-first of March. |

- The first of the month is **el primero**, although **el uno** is quite often heard: **el primero (uno) de abril**.

- You can ask and state the date in two ways.

| *¿Qué fecha es? –Es* el veintitrés de abril. *¿A cuántos estamos? –Estamos a* veintitrés de abril. | *What's the date?* –*It's* the twenty-third of April. |

On a date is expressed by simply using the definite article [➤21c(v)].

| ¿Qué fecha vamos a Caracas? –Vamos *el* diez de enero. | (On) what date do we go to Caracas? –We're going *on the* tenth of January. |

- The date expressed without naming the month is usually preceded by **el día**.

| Vamos a Caracas *el día diez.* | We're going to Caracas *on the tenth.* |

30d   *Years*

Years are expressed in exactly the same way as ordinary cardinal numbers.

1994   **mil novecientos noventa y cuatro**
2002   **dos mil dos**

Months are linked to a year by **de**.

| El diez de enero *de 1995.* | The tenth of January *1995.* |

- Note also:

Este manual se publicó *en 1993.*	This handbook was published *in 1993.*

Antes de Jesucristo (antes de J.C.) B.C.
Después de Jesucristo (después de J.C.) A.D.

G

INDEX

Index

W   warnings 15b (ii)
weather 8h (i), 22c (iii)
weights and measures 21c (v) (F)
what? 23g (ii)
whatever 16c (vii) (D)
what if...? 16h (v)
whenever 16c (vii) (A)
where? 27b (iii)
whether...or not 16c (viii)
which? 21b, 23g (iii)
which one? 23g (iii)
whoever 16c (vii) (C)
why? 27b (v)
word order 4g, 27c
would 14e (ii)

Y   **-y-** 2c (iii) (D)
y 5a (i), 28a (C)
ya no 27a (ii)
years 30d
your 21g (ii)